"If you're looking for a clear and balanced picture of America's spiritual landscape, this is it. George Gallup, Jr. and Timothy Jones use solid polling data to portray the current state of religion in America and to point the church in a direction that will help it become a major player in the shaping of the twenty-first century."

—*Peggy Wehmeyer*
Religion Correspondent
ABC News

"George Gallup, Jr. has his finger on the ever-changing spiritual pulse of this nation. This in-depth look at issues which will affect the American spiritual journey in the new millennium leaves the reader challenged, surprised, and optimistic that a renewal of the spirit holds promise for positive change in a world full of need."

—*Millard Fuller*
Founder and President
Habitat for Humanity International

THE
NEXT
American Spirituality

T H E

NEXT

AMERICAN SPIRITUALITY

FINDING GOD IN THE TWENTY–FIRST CENTURY

GEORGE GALLUP, JR.
TIMOTHY JONES

Cook Communications

Victor is an imprint of
Cook Communications Ministries, Colorado Springs, Colorado 80918
Cook Communications, Paris, Ontario
Kingsway Communications, Eastbourne, England

Cover Design: Koechel Peterson & Associates
Interior Design: Pat Miller
Editor: Greg Clouse

Library of Congress Cataloging-in-Publication Data
Gallup, George, 1930-
   The next American spirituality : finding God in the twenty-first century /
   George Gallup, Jr., Timothy Jones.
      p.cm.
   Includes bibliographical references.
   ISBN 0-78143-316-9
      1. United States—Religion—1960- 2. United States—Religion—
Forecasting. I. Jones, Timothy. II. Title.

BL2525 .G347 2000
200'.973'09051101—dc21   99-088255

1 2 3 4 5 6 7 8 9 10 Printing / Year 04 03 02 01 00

TABLE OF CONTENTS

To Kinny, my prayer partner and soul mate.

—G.G.

To Abram, Micah, and Bekah Jones, faithful carriers of the next American spirituality.

—T.J.

ACKNOWLEDGMENTS

O NCE AGAIN, IT is my pleasure to collaborate on a book with Timothy Jones, who has the great facility to convert cold survey data into clear, lively, and well-documented narrative.

I would also like to express my appreciation to Heidi Hintermeyer, who helped to develop the questionnaire for the "Twenty-four-Hour Spiritual Practice Survey" and to interpret the results.

— G. G.

I AM GRATEFUL for George Gallup, Jr.'s seasoned insight into American culture that made collaborating on this book a rich and illuminating experience.

Thanks, too, to Richard Kew, who provided valuable perspective.

— T. J.

INTRODUCTION

"The search for life's Anchor simply can't be viewed as weird anymore. It's gone from California fringe to national mainstream."

—FAITH POPCORN [1]

WHAT WOULD BRING more than a thousand city-toughened New Yorkers—including ex-cons and recovering addicts—to a Brooklyn church on a Tuesday night? Surely not a prayer meeting.

But prayer, says Brooklyn Tabernacle pastor Jim Cymbala, has become a mainstay of the thriving, multiracial church. Every Tuesday night, when the agenda holds little but two hours of fervent prayer for the city, the church, and the world, members pack the balcony and spill out into the foyer. The congregation, once tiny, depressed, and barely holding on, is convinced the explanation for its flourishing ministries is spiritual. "The earliest church," Cymbala explains, referring to the first-century apostles meeting in a Jerusalem upper room, "was born not in a clever sermon, but in a prayer meeting."

Stories like Brooklyn Tabernacle's may become more common in America. Americans seem to be praying more. Measurably higher numbers say they want to grow spiritually. Interest in the "spiritual life" has registered on indicator after indicator of cultural attention (about which we will say more later). While churchgoing may decline in some regions, while secularism continues to pervade much of our public life, we believe a change is already in the offing. A turn in the church (and indeed, in the culture) is profoundly altering the tenor of our times. "Spirituality is back almost with a vengeance," writes historian of modern religion Martin Marty. Never in recent memory has spirituality seemed to be so much on people's minds.

And the ferment and activity show no signs of abating. We expect more of the same. Amid healthy expressions and bogus claims, whether life-changing or flaky, whatever its warm promise and its sometime quirkiness, spirituality is here to stay.

Of course, there are limits to what anyone can forecast. "Prediction is very hard," as the common person's sage, Yogi Berra, puts it, "especially when it's about the future." Especially when it concerns a time of rapid, sometimes overwhelming, change. Massive transitions affect every aspect of life, including religious faith and spiritual practice. What consultant Tom Sine calls "the lively edge of what God is doing in our world" defies compartmentalizing.[2] In a real sense, then, we are not about predicting here as much as laying out compelling possibilities. We are offering glimpses of what will likely be, and what, if we are prepared, certainly can be.

Of course, we live and breathe and move amid forces whose impact we cannot fully discern in the present, much less the future. Who can say how youth violence and family disintegration or secularism and self-indulgent consumerism will counteract the quiet witness of churches, the hours of Habitat for Humanity volunteering, the Bible studies and worship services, the steady efforts of teachers and lawyers and maintenance workers and ministers? We are simply not given to know some of tomorrow's realities. But we see clear outlines emerging on the millennial horizon.

We will describe and document a number of edges of change in our culture, particularly those born of spirituality and religious renewal. These have relevance not only for what *is* and what will *come,* but also for how we can—now—respond to unprecedented opportunities and powerful challenges. We will suggest how leaders and influencers as well as "just plain folks" can make a difference. This we will do through stories, survey data, verbatim interviews, and informed prescriptions.

We will discuss how, for example, a deepened hunger for personal experience and felt faith will shape how people choose their congregations—and if they opt for church at all. We need to be aware of such ferment lest we forget to feed the soul and only recycle tired programs that fulfill fewer and fewer people.

Or, to cite another instance, while concern for the soul is out of the closet and even trendy, all that passes for spirituality in our culture will not stand the test of time or authentic practice. Many are finally discovering religion to be a matter of heart, not just rote (we will show why). But we will also show how contemporary spirituality can resemble a grab bag of random experiences that does little more than promise to make our eyes mist up or our heart warm. We need perspective to separate the junk food from the wholesome, the faddish from the truly transforming.

In yet another instance, for the first time in history, lengthening lifespans mean that up to seven generations (depending how you measure) live side by side. The "generation gap" of the sixties and seventies will have nothing on what is to come. Can we learn how to communicate cross-generationally? Will a "one-size-fits-all" approach to nurturing faith work amid the growing segmentation of age cohorts? Will we learn to pass along our faith to young people, many of whom already feel alienated and marginalized from mainstream culture and traditional religious communities? Will we capitalize on the incredibly powerful spiritual search of the young?

And what should we make of the advent of cyberspace and the vast interconnectedness of the World Wide Web? What *The Wall Street*

Journal recently termed "spirituality's controversial new frontier,"[3] is only beginning to shape perceptions and experiences of community. Will it continue to radically alter how people communicate and relate? If the nineties' explosive growth in the medium is any indication, even the next decade will usher in startling shifts. Will we know how to use technology's new tools both aggressively and appropriately? Will we be savvy to the dangers?

And this is just a sampling of the issues to be explored in this book. We will also draw a portrait of three groups that will shape the twenty-first century, three groups that to the surprise of many hold the key to lasting change. Knowing of their potential will do much to help us make room for and maximize their impact. We will offer suggestions for faith communities eager to reach out to the disenfranchised. We will assess the growing implication of the new globalization affecting our everyday lives. We will prescribe new patterns of community and outreach, faith-sharing and nurture. We will profile people whose spirituality is more than warm sentiment, but a life-changing, even culture-shaping, reality.

Twenty-four Hours that Move the Nation

To look at where spirituality has been and what it is, especially with an eye to discern how we can make a difference in the new climate, we will rely on years of polling data, wide reading, and careful cultural analysis. But those elements alone take us only so far.

Profiling America's next spirituality means examining what spiritual practice looks like up close, day in, day out. As we have looked ahead we have wondered, *What is the daily shape of faith behind the public expressions? How do people experience God in everyday life?* The George H. Gallup Institute conducted an extensive survey of Americans. We queried their daily habits—how and when they sense God's presence, experience indescribable joy, know despair, turn to prayer, help a neighbor. We specifically asked a representative sample what happened in the *last twenty-four hours,* believing this to give us the most sharply focused snapshots of what happens in the spiritual lives of Americans. While surveys typically record opinion and attitudes, our goal in this study was to probe deeper, to go to the bedrock of spiritual experience and actual practice. Within broad limits, we in effect entered into the homes and private longings of Americans.

Perhaps you have wondered if personal faith is alive and well in Americans' day-to-day lives. We uncovered unsettling, startling, and ultimately encouraging answers: we will show how a vast majority say they have a philosophy of life or rules that guide daily life. You might be surprised to learn how many (in this case, how few) consulted a psychic hotline or read their horoscope, while many more said they had read the Bible. Two-thirds said they had prayed in the last twenty-four hours. Almost half claimed to have had "a strong sense of God's presence" and said they "went out of their way" to help someone in need for religious or spiritual reasons. How many say they feel life is empty or meaningless? Surprisingly few. When faced with difficulty and discouragement, a majority claim to turn to "God, a higher power, the inner self, or Jesus Christ." We asked more than "yes" or "no" questions, including eliciting definitions of the word *spirituality*. The definitions give reason for pause, as well as satisfaction. We also asked what people would in turn ask God, if they could. The answers were as varied as they were fascinating.

This twenty-four-hour survey reveals more than where Americans sit. It suggests stirrings of change and rumors of things to come. We can tease out of the data arresting glimpses. We can mine from it prescriptions for how people of faith can respond to a rapidly changing world. A full third of the book will explore concrete implications of our vision for what will be. That is why we will present "futuribles"—a phrase common in France—to suggest what is possible. [4] Throughout we want to emphasize, *This is the world on the way—and tomorrow as it can be.*

We approach the task with more than mild interest. While we strongly suspect that the new spiritual seeking will flourish, with far-reaching effects for our society and the world, we are not sanguine about its inevitability. Much hinges on people seeing ahead and seizing the moment. We will therefore demonstrate why spirituality *matters*—perhaps more than ever. Concern for spiritual health, we argue, is no exercise in pious rhetoric. Because so many of our national problems have spiritual roots, not simply political and sociological causes, a renewal of the spirit holds promise for positive change that reaches into every arena of life. For potential to become even partly substance will require prayer, work, and clear-eyed insight. People of faith are uniquely equipped for that very mandate. Our nation has been battered by a crisis not so much of politics or education as of soul; the answers must include recourse to larger, deeper resources. The renewal of our churches, the restoration of our families, and the reclamation of our cities and towns will require a more profound spiritual grounding.

The Tribe of Issachar

In a different setting, centuries ago, when the Israelites joined their king, David, in battle, we read in 1 Chronicles 12 of the tribe of Issachar, "who understood the times and knew what Israel should do" (1 Chronicles 12:32). We do well, too, to understand our times. As a nation, as believers, as community volunteers, as interested onlookers, we gaze ahead, not to speculate about what we do not need to know, but to discern where our culture stands and to where it runs. Such looking ahead is not like gazing into a crystal ball; it is more like peering to a morning horizon, reading the portents of the approaching day, the signs of the times Jesus talked about. Only that will allow us the vantage point of what Tom Sine calls "leading with foresight." Only then will we not miss dramatic opportunities. Only then will we not fumble for lack of strategies. Only then will we pray wisely.

Not everyone will agree with our suggestions and forecasts, of course, even if they be informed ones. Nor should they! By sharing our findings and suggesting future scenarios we invite other ideas and debate, other analyses and best-guesses. The important thing is that we observe, talk, pray, and plan for changes to come. We can no longer design our programs, reach out to people around us, lay out our next steps, and wait for God's tomorrow relying only on what has been. Our age of accelerated change vividly shows us that the future will not simply be an extension of the past. It will be a new thing—ultimately God's new thing. We pray that this book helps to ready you, and a waiting world, for the sobering and wonderful realities ahead.

AMERICA'S EPIC SOUL QUEST

*"If the world has not approached its end, it has reached
a major watershed . . . equal in history to the turn from
the Middle Ages to the Renaissance. It will demand from
us a spiritual blaze."*
—ALEKSANDR SOLZHENITSYN AT HARVARD UNIVERSITY

W E WISH WE could tear out the images from our national
memory. For a few days in April 1999, horrific scenes dom-
inated every newscast. Radio programs, Web sites, and hallway office conversations bore gruesome details of high school
students and a coach mown down by gunfire, and more left blood-
ied. A well-to-do enclave of 35,000 residents southwest of Denver
near the foothills of the Rockies, a town dotted with golf courses
where many never bothered to lock their doors at night, became syn-
onymous with grim violence. *Littleton,* notes Martin Marty, became
a code word for trauma, much like Pearl Harbor and Jonestown.

Ken Ross would love to forget the images, too. The Episcopal minister serves a church of mostly young professionals, less than three

miles from the scene of carnage at Columbine High. Until a couple of years ago, his fledgling congregation met in a trailer. With attendance flourishing, they had recently dedicated their new sanctuary with great joy. Then Ken watched his community blanketed with pain and anguish. His own ten-year-old asked, "God knew this was going to happen; why didn't He stop it?" At thirty-five, Ken has blond hair and slender, boyish looks (someone once nicknamed him Doogie Howser). But his pastoral work has required grave, mature wisdom. While none of the youth in his church were killed, one high schooler watched a friend die. Everyone was left reeling.

Along with the rest of the watching nation, Ken noticed immediately another story behind the anguished headlines. Through the accounts of teenage angst in Colorado, through the ensuing debates about gun control and parental responsibility, there wove a surprising thread: the way people turned, sometimes desperately, to faith. Someone cowering with fellow students, the news media reported, hiding from gunshot in the choir room of Columbine High, whispered, "Who's religious? Anybody in here religious?" "The huddled students," continued reporter Nancy Gibbs for *Time* magazine, "started to pray, very, very quietly." [1] Across the nation the word *prayer* was broadcast into living rooms or featured in articles with remarkable frequency. "With each passing day of shock and grief," wrote Gibbs in *Time,* "you could almost hear the church bells tolling in the background, calling the country to a different debate." [2]

And a community and the nation publicly turned to faith in remarkable ways. Littleton-area high school students began meeting for prayer vigils. A contractor from Aurora, Illinois, built fifteen wooden crosses in his garage and drove to Littleton to put them on a hill overlooking the school, creating a makeshift, open-air shrine. One eyewitness reported that people wrote nasty slogans on the crosses memorializing the two gunmen, but the gathered teenagers begged them not to. When the sloganeers persisted, the young people broke out in a soft, a cappella rendition of "Amazing Grace." Ken Ross appeared on the memorial site on a couple of occasions, each time bearing a case of almost two hundred Bibles. Each time the Bibles were gone within an hour, many given to unbelieving teenagers searching for answers, eager to talk about God.

In the days after the shooting, the line between secular TV and religious broadcasting blurred. Ross tells how local coverage accorded students amazing freedom to talk about their Christian faith. One student interviewed on the evening news told of taking cover under a table, pulling in with him fellows students, praying in "tongues," as charismatic Christians call it, and telling them about Jesus. "After a couple of weeks, that changed," Ken recalls. "I saw a change of tone, a return to less explicitly spiritual reporting. But a window of opportunity opened for a brief time." Worldwide, CNN televised memorial services with uncensored stories of evangelical faith. According to Darrell Scott, father of shooting victim Rachel Scott, producers told him the funeral services in churches captured CNN's largest viewer audience ever. And of course, Americans heard of Cassie Bernall, a once-rebellious teenager reportedly asked at gunpoint if she believed in God. Soon marketers began selling T-shirts and paraphernalia emblazoned with her last words as a kind of slogan testimony: "Yes, I believe in God." Strangely, anachronistically in our do-as-convenient culture, commentators revived the religious vocabulary of martyrdom. And still the questions about faith and deeper resources lingered, affecting the community, even the nation.

In a different way, Americans were soon to mourn yet again, stunned in just three months by the death of young John F. Kennedy, Jr., a tragedy that reminded Americans of the waves of shock sent out from his father's assassination decades earlier. Here again appeared another subtext striking to observers of American culture: a country turning stubbornly, in this supposedly secular age, to the rites and comforts of religious faith. On our television screens we viewed makeshift secular shrines (the piling up of flowers at the couple's apartment doorstep, for instance), heard traditional eulogies, saw priests with their clerical collars in clear view. St. Patrick's Cathedral, the Church of St. Thomas More, Christ Cathedral bespoke a more classical, "high" church tone than the evangelical fervor of Littleton, but again and again there was faith: Anne Freeman, mother of Carolyn Bessette Kennedy and Lauren Bessette, read from a book of sermons. A Kennedy cousin recited the Twenty-third Psalm. In a time of grief it seemed only natural for people to turn to the comforts of faith.

But Aren't These Secular Times?

The accent on spiritual realities stands out all the more because it comes when many lament the erosion of religion's influence. Hasn't a virulent antipathy to Christianity and traditional faith won the day? Institutions seem wary of (even hostile to) public expressions of faith, leading one Yale Law School professor to dub ours a "culture of disbelief." [3] Using more philosophical categories, sociologist Max Weber argued that we have witnessed "the disenchantment of the world." Writers speak of the disappearance of Christendom, of how Christianity has been disestablished, knocked off the throne of even civic respect. Common wisdom has it that for many, especially the rising generations, organized religion seems passé, dated. Some see churches and other religious institutions as out of touch. On one episode of *The Simpsons*, son Bart asks his father, Homer, what his religious beliefs are. "You know, the one with all the well-meaning rules that don't work in real life. Uh, Christianity." [4] Entertainment media still delight to portray the faithful as buffoons or bigots. Moral flabbiness and religious relativism, or a militant religionlessness, pervade our institutions. Even when television portrays religious faith sympathetically, it rarely goes deep; Peter Steinfels of *The New York Times* recently wrote of TV's "very short theological attention span."

We will argue in this book that communities of faith—and our culture—nevertheless stand poised at a threshold fraught with

promise. We believe that in the new century the church, God's people all over the world, can play a key role in reshaping life as we
know it. Not because the calendar pages signal the dawn of a new
millennium, not because "care of the soul" is trendy, but because we
are witnessing a culture striking out on a quest of seismic proportions. Ours represents a profound time to offer ministry and invite
people to belief. Already, the grieving patterns of Littleton and the
Kennedy aftermath mirror an underlying shift of consciousness.
True, part of what we see there is simply a residue of old traditions.
But the spiritual dynamic underlying this shift has caught the attention of church leaders and secular observers alike. The erosion of
religion's moorings in recent decades seems
to have done little to dampen spirituality. In
some ways it may have intensified it. The percentage of Americans who "completely agree"
that "prayer is an important part of my daily
life" rose from 41 percent in 1987 to 53 percent in 1997, an increase of twelve percentage
points. Those who "completely agree" that
they never doubt the existence of God rose
eleven points in the same ten years. Our survey of Americans' daily spiritual practices,

> The percentage of Americans who "complete-ly agree" that "prayer is an important part of my daily life" rose from 41 percent in 1987 to 53 percent in 1997, an increase of twelve per-centage points. Those who "completely agree" that they never doubt the exis-tence of God rose eleven points in the same ten years.

limiting ourselves to what they actually *did* in a twenty-four-hour
period, only confirms what the broader polls have been indicating.

Even Americans' stance toward organized religion is faring better,
reversing a downward slide. The Princeton Religion Research Center
Index, [5] a kind of Dow-Jones Industrial Average of religion that measures eight key religious beliefs and practices, has recently begun an
upward turn. Through questions about confidence and religion,
church and clergy, and membership levels, we have seen steady rises.
It registered a sharp rise in 1997. Further, the percentage of Americans who think religion is increasing its influence on American life
climbed a remarkable twelve points between August of 1997 and
January of 1998, to the highest point in twelve years.

As we enter a new millennium, religious belief seems poised to thrive and flourish. "Religion makes a comeback," declared a *New York Times Magazine* lead story. "America has outgrown its 'take it or leave it' attitude toward religion," the article continued. "Now, even people without faith are looking for God." The article led with a sentence that seems hardly at home in the urbane newspaper: "Is America in the grip of a religious revival?" [6] We see a turning again and anew to the rock-hard comforts of faith. One can almost understand the impatience of one of the respondents to our twenty-four-hour survey. When asked "Do you feel the need in your life to experience spiritual growth?" the retired Protestant schoolteacher blurted, "Doesn't everybody?" That seems to sum up the mood of our times.

Even counselors and psychiatrists, sometimes stereotyped as uniformly wary of a faith dimension, promote spiritual health. In 1990, two researchers surveyed members of the American Psychological Association about their approach to religion and psychology. Nearly all said they had assessed their patients' religious background. Almost a third said they had recommended religious or spiritual books, 24 percent prayed privately for a patient, and 7 percent prayed with a client. [7] Medical schools now teach the health benefits of spirituality. Hebert Benson, M.D., directs a class for the The Harvard Medical School of Continuing Education called "Spirituality and Healing in Medicine" that each year attracts a thousand physicians, psychologists, clergy, nurses, social workers, and others. About sixty medical schools now offer related classes, up from the mid-1990s, when only three did. [8]

Indeed, while some at the beginning of the twentieth century predicted the eclipse of religion by its close, few forecasts now seem more ludicrous. Decades ago one radical German theologian declared that it was impossible for anyone who believed in electricity to believe in miracles. Time has shown his folly. Faith is in the air. *The New York Times Magazine* recently reported a Gallup survey that indicated that 96 percent of the population said they believed in God. And while nearly 60 percent saw religion itself declining in influence, that represents fewer than the year before, suggesting a more positive trend. Likewise, the prominence of faith in the Littleton aftermath comes as no accident; the town has hosted for years more than its share of thriving evangelical churches. Bible clubs flourish on the town's high school campuses. Littleton is not alone.

Across the board, as you will soon see, surveys confirm a remarkable rise in spiritual concern: the percentage of Americans who say they feel the need to experience spiritual growth has risen sharply, up twenty-four points, in just four years. Our twenty-four-hour survey—asking what did you *do* in the last day, with its queries about actual practice, not simply good intentions—tells us that *two-thirds of Americans have prayed within the last twenty-four hours!* (And these are no mere panicked cries for help out of a jam or a request for a new VCR.) An encouraging proportion say they seek God's guidance and help for daily choices. People seem drawn to deeper resources. For a time angels were trendy. Even as we write, a long-running television prime-time television program attests to people "Touched by an Angel." Books on soul and spiritual experience are all the publishing rage. Our schoolteacher respondent, when asked, "During the last twenty-four hours, did you happen to pray?" said, "Yes—all day!"

Who would have thought that cocktail parties and boardrooms would become places where we talk about our personal spiritual strivings openly and heatedly? One Lutheran layperson, a rancher from South Dakota, was getting dressed for a workout at a health club.

One Lutheran layperson, a rancher from South Dakota, was getting dressed for a workout at a health club. He happened to mention to his locker mate his plan to attend a spiritual retreat on Thomas Merton, the late monk and social activist. Suddenly two other men in the locker room, both lawyers, turned to him. "We're reading books on spirituality," they said. One was on his thirteenth Merton book. The South Dakotan told the story to his fellow retreat attenders, incredulous.

He happened to mention to his locker mate his plan to attend a spiritual retreat on Thomas Merton, the late monk and social activist. Suddenly two other men in the locker room, both lawyers, turned to him. "We're reading books on spirituality," they said. One was on his thirteenth Merton book. The South Dakotan told the story to his fellow retreat attenders, incredulous. While in many ways the foundations of religious tradition show themselves shakier than in the past, notes Princeton sociologist Robert Wuthnow, "[J]udging from newspapers and television, Americans' fascination with spirituality has been escalating dramatically." 9

Is part of what we see the turning away from the unworkable philosophies of hedonism, narcissism, and materialism? Our travels abroad tell us that people in a wide range of societies manifest a new hunger for healing of mind, body, and soul. And America, one of the most religious countries of the Western world, is no exception. "If the gods of secularism are now joining the gods of Marxism in crumbling on the sidelines," writes inner-city minister Dennett Buettner, "perhaps that is only because the two were so similar that when one set fell the other was bound to follow." In some ways, at least, our penchant for activism and an impatient "can-do" response to every problem is giving way to a quieter, more contemplative disposition. Suddenly prayer seems not so quaint or out of reach.

It is possible, of course, that the recovery of spirituality will go the way of other fads and short-lived movements. Might it become just a blip on the cultural radar screen? Who can say for sure it won't? Institutional forms of faith continue to take hard knocks (witness the T-shirt emblazoned with the words, "Lord Jesus, please save me from your followers"). People of Christian faith remain captive to much of the consumerism, self-absorption, and addictions of the wider culture. But from analysis of decades of polling and the twenty-four-hour survey (explored in detail in later chapters), we believe we are witnessing more than a mere mild indulgence of spiritual curiosity. We observe instead a profound opportunity to engage a wider culture in serious conversations about faith, even to echo through our times the centuries-old invitation of Jesus, to come and follow.

For what is happening around us is opening people to genuine searching. One of the authors once asked Martin Marty, professor of modern Christianity at the University of Chicago, if he felt the modern soul fascination was authentic. "The hunger is always authentic," he answered. "It's just that you can feed it with Twinkies or with broccoli." Much of what happens will hinge on how people of faith, empowered by the Holy Spirit, seize the moment. Much will depend on the church rising to the opportunity culture is giving it. Much turns on the church recovering its mission not only to program but also to pray; to do more than stay busy with activities but also to nurture intimacy with God. Religious communities need to reclaim a core mission to lead people to love God and love their neighbors as themselves. If the church can recover its role as a place of belonging and nurture and honest seeking after God, remarkable things can happen.

Already people in the church are being quickened to pray for revival in their midst. Already faith communities are recovering a mission to lead people into experiences of true community, not just routine activities. Already courageous ministers call their people to face-to-face interaction with society's needy. Will it mean a spilling over into culture of the spiritual fruit of a Great Awakening? Will society as we know it feel the lasting effects? Will the "saints among us," to recall the title of our earlier book—those believers whose faith makes a true and lasting difference in the world—continue to flourish? [10]

The Bad News

Perhaps even these questions sound too glib. Just because Americans claim they are more spiritual does not make them so. Is the church really rediscovering its spiritual moorings—or just engaging in retreat from seemingly insoluble problems? Is American culture really being swept by a tidal wave of soulful seeking? Some are not so sure.

Evidence to the contrary certainly abounds. Who cannot point to gaps in what Americans believe and how they behave? By some counts, church attendance has yet to reverse solidly its downward trend. Certainly mainline denominations (such as the Methodists, Episcopalians, and Presbyterians) have taken a membership hammering. Instead of attending church, some turn to makeshift prophets and secular priests. When people do profess spiritual interest, there seems to be plenty of "me-ism" mixed in.

There are other disheartening signs. In polls on biblical literacy, half of those describing themselves as Christians are unable to name who delivered the Sermon on the Mount. Many Americans cannot name the reason for celebrating Easter or what the Ten Commandments are. People think the name of Noah's wife was Joan, as in *Joan of Ark.* One Nevada politician, who proposed a tax on gambling but realized he faced the state's most powerful industry, told his constituents that he didn't want to kill his Goliath-like opponent, just "hurt him a little . . . like King David in the Bible." Whose Bible was he reading (or in this case, not reading)? [11] (More on this in the next chapter.)

Secularism continues to define us in many ways; history textbooks routinely omit reference to religion's influence on the early Pilgrim settlers or the Rev. Martin Luther King. A national survey of journalists and historians recently asked them to list the top one hundred news stories of the twentieth century. The atom bomb, Hitler, President Kennedy's assassination made the list, as expected. What was surprising was the near absence of religion. Movements and events that precipitated cultural shifts were simply missing: the Scopes trial in 1925, symbolizing America's changing relationship between science and religion; Vatican II, that seismic shift in modern Catholicism; the Holocaust, so seminal to Jewish consciousness; the rise of Pentecostalism and reemergence of Islam. [12] Public school systems, anxious about legal entanglement, have largely turned a cold shoulder to the practice of faith. Prayer and religion, even nonsectarian moral guidelines, have been leached out of our public life. Anyone who has been laughed at for articulating his or her religious beliefs could be forgiven for doubting that spirituality is hot.

And we see constant reminders of moral failure, if not headlong decline. Political leaders flagrantly transgress moral and professional standards. Television has become a moral wasteland. Two-thirds of adults in the U.S. say the country's moral and cultural values have changed for the worse since the 1960s. It is not hard to understand why. Paul Weyrich, president of the Free Congress Foundation and a founding father of the Moral Majority, now says that traditionalists "have lost the culture war." The nation is caught up, he argues, "in a cultural collapse of historic proportions, a collapse so great that it simply overwhelms politics." While his dismal assessment has been hotly debated, it is easy to understand the sentiment.

And should not a nation begun in the spirit of One who called people to love God and love neighbor show more humane progress? Our economic standard of living continues to rise, but few would argue that our compassion index has soared. The gap between the comfortably wealthy and the needy poor widens. Indeed, the situation has gotten so bad that many lose hope or cave in to cynicism. For the first time in a half-century of surveys on Americans' top national concerns, a Gallup poll conducted in 1999 revealed that "ethics, morality, and family decline" led the list at 18 percent. Concern over "crime and violence" registered a close second at 17 percent. In another survey, not quite half recently said they were pessimistic about the future of moral and ethical standards. "Americans are worried that their country is backsliding," writes commentator David Broder. "Despite the best economy in most people's memory, a spate of public opinion polling affirms that most voters are deeply concerned about the moral climate and are searching for ways to restore what they see as lost values." [13] The title of his editorial says much: "The National Mood Has Darkened." As one friend of ours puts it, "Every time you

For the first time in a half-century of surveys on Americans' top national concerns, a Gallup poll conducted in 1999 revealed that "ethics, morality, and family decline" led the list at 18 percent.

pick up a newspaper you read some new travesty of truth, justice, or integrity."

Americans know instinctively that much around us feeds our moral laxness and spiritual aimlessness. Here is just a sampling of the "bad news" that seems to throw into question the evidence for a spiritual awakening and renewal of society, evidence that will sound wearyingly familiar to a careful observer of national life:

■ *Unsettling violence.* A few decades ago Americans would almost never name crime among their community's top problems, but now it ranks foremost in communities of all sizes. People perceive increasing threats from assault and killing, of which Littleton is simply one example. While lately there have been some encouraging signs of youth violence declining, recent decades overall have hosted a sharp upturn in various kinds of violence. Twenty-eight percent of teens say they are aware of peers who have carried or regularly carry guns and knives when they are in school. Guns are so prevalent that American children under fifteen are fifteen times more likely to die by accidental shooting than in the other twenty-five industrialized nations combined. Surveys indicate that child abuse and sexual abuse are far worse than official figures suggest. Alcohol, drug abuse, and a decline in values breed more violence.

■ *Corruption in leadership.* Politicians score low on the public's ethics scale, feeding a growing disillusionment with political (and indeed all) institutions. As reflected in the decline in voter participation in national elections over the past four decades, people feel disenfranchised from the political and electoral process, disappointed by the politicians they elect, trust, and feel betrayed by.

■ *Lifestyle gaps.* A cluster of moral and theological shortcomings seemingly throws into question the transforming power of religious beliefs. Between what Americans profess and manifest lie gaps of knowledge, behavior, and ethics. When our nation's four to five hundred thousand clergy address their congregations each week, they face people whose choices contradict their values. "The great disconnect," someone has called it. Church leaders face young people who must live off their disinheritance—offspring of absentee parents who never instructed them in faith and virtue. Clergy preach to boomers who believe in angels but cheat on taxes, college students who pray but regularly get drunk. [14]

■ *Alcohol and drug abuse.* The percentage of Americans who say that drinking has been a problem in their homes—one-fourth—has reached the highest point in recent decades. Gallup surveys show that nearly half of teens think drinking is a problem among their peers. The proportion rises among teens ages sixteen and seventeen. Sixteen percent worry about their own use of hard drugs. Much crime feeds off these addictions.

■ *Poverty.* While the standard of living in America has increased dramatically over the past half-century, the nation remains plagued by pockets of poverty. A review of homelessness in fifty cities found that in virtually every city, the city's official estimated number of homeless people greatly exceeded the number of emergency shelter and transitional housing spaces. [15] Gallup polls show that as many as one-fourth of the public (and nearly half of nonwhites) have said that there were times in the past twelve months they did not have enough money to buy the food, clothing, or medical supplies they needed. One can write off some of that as Americans' inflated expectations and overly pampered lifestyles, but not all, not when one widely quoted study found that 6.5 percent (representing 12 million adults nationwide) had been literally homeless at some point in their lives.

■ *Racism.* Although the income, housing, and education gaps between whites and blacks have been closing in recent decades, blacks continue to report racial bias on many fronts. They are not hopeful about racial relations in the future. Rioting and outbreaks of violence in our inner cities, along with hate crimes directed at members of ethnic minorities, continue to show that we do not live in a classless, color-blind society. The number of Web sites devoted to slandering racial and other groups has mushroomed. Writes a reporter for *Time* magazine: "According to Rabbi Abraham Cooper, associate dean of the Simon Wiesenthal Center in Los Angeles, the number of hate websites has ballooned from one to more than 2,000 in the past four years." [16]

■ *Family breakdown.* Six out of every ten new marriages will not last and our culture seems cavalier about its commitment to marriage and the priority of family. Too many children grow up in households with absentee parents. Promiscuity and "the twin threats of AIDS and unwanted pregnancy make teen sex more complicated—and danger-ous—than before." [17]

■ *Consumerism and materialism.* As one of the richest and most consumptive nations in the world, America seems blithely unaware of its self-indulgence when compared to other cultures. Americans, when assessing their contentment level, compare them-selves to their more affluent neighbors, not their poorer international counterparts. These attitudes even take on a kind of religious signifi-cance. Pastor and writer Mark Buchanan speaks of the "Cult of the Next Thing." "It has its own litany of sacred words: *more, you deserve it, new, faster, cleaner, brighter.* It has its own deep-rooted liturgy: *charge it, instant credit, no down-payment . . . no inter-est for three months.* It has its own preachers, evangelists, prophets, and apostles: ad men, pitchmen, celebrity sponsors. . . . It has its own ecstatic experiences: the spending spree. . . . Most of us spend more time with advertisements than with Scripture." [18]

So What Really Is Happening?

We believe that such problems do not contradict the presence of spiritual renewal, but rather they help explain it. The limits of human "progress," the flat aftertaste of an unbridled pursuit of affluence, and the callousness of nations whose civil wars sicken us with video footage of atrocities, all have driven people to look within and above themselves. Is it any accident that the percentage of persons who say they have given a lot of thought to the basic meaning and value of their lives has grown in the last years of the tumultuous twentieth century? Indeed, it has shot from 58 percent in 1985 to 69 percent in the late nineties. Argues Princeton sociologist Robert Wuthnow,

"Much of Americans' current religious behavior can be understood as a result of [the] new confrontation with secularity. . . . They are not marching steadfastly into a secular age but are reshaping deep religious traditions in ways that help make sense of the new realities of their lives." [19] Our public tendency toward secularism, in other words, seems only to have increased our spiritual longings.

As we face increasingly complex times—problems that run out of control, such as pollution, violence in the schools, poverty, hunger, environmental devastation—solutions appear insurmountable by recourse to our own strength. [20] When addictions leave people feeling powerless, it is no accident that they turn to a Higher Power. When data threatens to overwhelm with information, we become desperate for wisdom to help us make our way through the overload.

At the same time, many of the old habits and customs have broken down, patterns that would have once let people turn to the church or religious traditions for help in solving the deeper dilemmas. In an earlier era, people might have turned to a matriarch or pastor or rabbi or other trusted mentor. Now many do not know where to turn. Dislocation routinely uproots families to follow job transfers and leaves people stranded, isolated. Stresses leave us feeling more and more hurried and harried. Our possessions seem to own us and our schedules regiment us. Amid such tumult, Americans speak of their spirituality growing while they perceive, at least until recently, religion's impact diminishing. As we will show in the next chapter, faith grows both more private and eclectic, more inwardly focused and less outwardly grounded. As a result, churches experience continuing decline and a seeming slide toward the cultural margins. With churches seeming more irrelevant, people grow more confused and more anxious in their seeking.

But we see another possibility. Americans are seeking ways to reestablish a connection to vital faith. An abiding restlessness, ultimately spiritual in essence, continues to drive them.

> Americans are seeking ways to reestablish a connection to vital faith. An abiding restlessness, ultimately spiritual in essence, continues to drive them. Author Leonard Sweet calls what is hitting postmodern culture a "spiritual tsunami."

Author Leonard Sweet calls what is hitting postmodern culture a "spiritual tsunami." This wave, he says, "will build without breaking for decades to come." [21] Is it too strong an image? Time will tell. Like a beach ball that you try to push under ocean water only to have it rocket back to the surface, the hunger for the divine pushes upward through our collective consciousness. Our innate spiritual hunger, for a time perhaps suppressed, ignored, explained away, refuses to go away. Religion may be falling on hard times. But spirituality has crashed secularism's party. One survey suggests that about 40 percent of Americans have had an unusual, life-changing spiritual experience. "If the 1980s were the decade where nothing was sacred," says one marketing analyst, "then this is the one when everything is." If much focus on the latter half of the twentieth century settled on outer space, will perhaps the focus on the first decades of the next century center on inner space? Many residents of Littleton, Colorado, aching from tragedy and desperate for inward resources, would agree.

> "If the 1980s were the decade where nothing was sacred," says one marketing analyst, "then this is the one when everything is." If much focus on the latter half of the twentieth century settled on outer space, will perhaps the focus on the first decades of the next century center on inner space?

And so would many young people there, whom pastor Ken Ross calls "more radical and willing to be committed than my own Generation X." How fascinating that years before the Littleton massacre, generation researchers William Strauss and Neil Howe argued that the "millennial" generation, including the class of 2000, would be a heroic generation. And it is hardly surprising that Sweet claims the spiritual tsunami "has hit the postmodern generations especially hard." [22] That it has strengthens our belief that the new spiritual electricity in the air will not lose its voltage soon. Too many young people have been galvanized by it. Too many of all age groups suffer the emptiness of soul brownouts. Americans seem ready for a fresh approach to universal heart hungers and soul needs that have never really gone away, only been ignored or brushed past. A breeze that feels wildly real and life-changing seems to be blowing. We can only wonder what sparks of renewal it will carry.

And while much of the impetus for spiritual seeking seems to come from outside the church (for the first time in this nation's history), Christians are already experiencing the tsunami's impact. Church leader after leader reports great and growing interest in more than a secondhand, long-distance relationship with God. Millions of American Christians are drawn to prayer meetings, spiritual growth weekends, and Bible study groups. Gatherings for prayer and extended periods of fasting have drawn record numbers. In the last year of the 1900s, as many as three million school-age young people and their teachers gathered for "See You at the Pole" prayer rallies at their school flagpoles. The examples abound. Friends of ours wrote a book in 1992 titled *New Millennium, New Church*, wherein they suggested there might be a rise of spirituality and formation movements during the 1990s, a "quiet revolution" that would continue to grow at the grassroots parish level throughout the remainder of the century. But now, says one of the authors, Richard Kew, "Oh my, how wrong we were! This [spirituality boom] has hardly been a quiet shifting of gears. It has been raucous, burgeoning uncontrollably like kudzu in the Southern summer." Clearly, something is going on.

As American's epic soul quest continues, our culture's spiritual curiosity in turn will present the church with an evangelistic moment. When have people in our culture ever been so open to conversation about angels or the afterlife? Even Jesus has hit the news with cover stories in news magazines and best-selling books. In the average modern person's mind, the *Christian* implications of those subjects are not clear, but culture's awakening spiritual curiosity presents us opportunities on a silver platter to make the connection, opportunities to discuss faith in Jesus Christ. And in the church, prayer and the spiritual life, heart religion and transforming faith, will have a chance to thrive. We have reason to be expectant, but most of all ready.

The Big Change

But the situation this time is no mere return to earlier eras of revival or Great Awakening. At the beginning of the twentieth century, the majority of Americans practiced their faith in at least a general framework that could be called Judeo-Christian. They went from cradle to grave in a specific religious tradition. Now people are less likely to turn to a church or religious institution, more apt to depend on self-help books or tips from talk shows to arrive at their beliefs. People enlist an assortment of religious influences, some wholesome, others bizarre, such as gun-toting militia groups or pagan-influenced Wicca (witchcraft). Some best-selling books, such as *Embraced by the Light* and *The Celestine Prophecy*, dish up odd amalgams of Eastern and Western, pagan and traditional, occult and Christian beliefs. The interest in angels provides a case in point: the topic of angels is decidedly biblical, more so than, say, Tarot cards, yet the New Age has adopted angels with a flourish, overlaying occult categories and practices. Others speak of Hindu reincarnation in the same breath with channeling the spirits of the departed and Christian ethical principles. A flourishing neo-paganism has once again captured the serious religious attention of thousands. The spiritual hunger will need tending, sorting out, discerning. It will take winsome invitations and articulate correction.

The situation is not unlike that faced by Augustine in the fourth century. While Augustine's milieu was officially Christian, paganism and polytheism still abounded in a number of towns where he lived. Christians tasted and dipped from this religion or that divinity. Roman myth got mixed with Christian theology. For many, this mix of myth and theology never did get sorted out. When Augustine was bishop he rebuked members of his congregation who said: "Just because I frequent idols and get advice from visionaries and fortune tellers, that does not mean I have left the church—I am a Catholic!" [23]

Not only is much of our culture's spiritual experimentation off-track, idolatries coexist and compete for Americans' spiritual affection.

Our society breeds consumers, spectators, and self-absorbed individuals, argues Dave Henderson in his book *Culture Shift.* [24] Is it any wonder that people in our churches approach their spiritual hungers expecting microwave convenience? John Mogabgab, editor the spiritual-life journal *Weavings,* warns of the danger of our "quickaholic" times, our "age of acceleration," as someone has called it. When such a tenor gets "imported into spiritual experience," he notes, "people may not experience what they hope for as quickly as they expect." They may hop from fad to fad. As we will explore in depth in the next chapter, Americans face constant temptations to pass over the wisdom of the ancients in favor of the guru of the month. In today's postmodern world, "spirituality" may as easily refer to the cult of the goddess, or to channeling occult spirits, as to the practice of historic Judeo-Christian piety.

Will the church learn how to communicate engagingly, persuasively in this milieu? That remains to be seen. And if, by the sovereign hand of God, revival does sweep the church, as it has in earlier eras, will it actively present what it finds to a seeking, searching world?

The Soul of a Nation

"One of the best rules of making forecasts," writes economist Sylvia Porter, "is to remember that whatever is to happen is happening already." That the generation of Littleton high school students instinctively turned very publicly to the vocabulary of religion and the practice of prayer confirms what polls show and what we expect to continue. Those young people's lives, punctuated by random violence, guided by both ancient values and contemporary currents, already profile America's next spirituality. What the Columbine generation believes and practices steadily shapes life as we will know it in the third millennium.

That the generation of Littleton high school students instinctively turned very publicly to the vocabulary of religion and the practice of prayer confirms what polls show and what we expect to continue.

If traditional faith and values showed up vividly in the ways we mourned our dead in 1999, they also show up in the day-to-day choices we make as we live. And just as the media coverage tells us that God has not been squeezed out of our daily life, not by a long shot, so the twenty-four-hour survey underscores that Americans are undeniably and increasingly concerned about matters of soul and spirit.

But the news has a sobering side, too. Littleton pastor Ken Ross tells of a Rwandan friend, a bishop in that war-torn nation. When tragedy struck at Columbine, Ken's African friend, witness to even more horrific bloodshed, warned him, "Right after a great tragedy, you will see many people 'get religion.' They even become hyper-spiritual. But after about three months, with the crisis over, they taper off. They don't want to hear any more of either suffering or God's redemptive grace." And that, Ken Ross admits, has begun to happen in Littleton. Many were changed for the better by the tragedy, he says, drawn to saving faith. But the window of opportunity closed soon after.

Our nation may face a similar fate. If the cultural tenor manifests unheard-of openness to spiritual realities, we cannot take it for granted. We have work to do. And a time-sensitive opportunity that should make us urgent.

In order to address our current circumstances, however, we cannot start with practical prescriptions. We need first to understand deeply our culture's longings and experiences—the promise and pitfalls of a newfound spirituality, to which we now turn our attention.

THE NEW SPIRITUALITY

"We are living in a secular society but a spiritual culture."
—AL WINSEMAN, OMAHA, NEBRASKA, PASTOR [1]

EW PHRASES BOTHER Marilyn McGuire more than *New Age.* The blonde grandmother, who orders her wardrobe from Eddie Bauer and looks younger than her sixty years, bristles at the pictures the term conjures up—the media stereotypes of healing crystals and pyramid power. Spirituality, however, is very important to her, she explains from her home on a island village northwest of Seattle.

And Marilyn McGuire certainly emphasizes a life of spiritual practice. Her windows open onto the Pacific and snowcapped vistas of Mount Rainier and Mount Baker, reminding her of creation's glories. Most mornings she and a friend greet the island's rustic beauty and salt-tanged air with 5:30 walks. To the accompaniment of seagulls' cries, she uses a wood-burning stove for heat and cooking, noting, "In this simpler setting, away from the bustle and noise, I find a sense of

peace and proximity to God that's crucial for me to function—
especially in a world that offers as many options and challenges as
ours." As she goes about her day administering her publishing and
book marketing organization, she will pray under her breath, "Let
the words of my mouth and the meditations of my heart be accept-
able to you, O God," echoing phrases from Isaiah and the *Book of
Common Prayer,* carryovers from her Episcopalian youth. "I am a
Christian," she will say when asked her religious preference.

Still, her beliefs range beyond traditional boundaries. She
believes, in fact, that she truly began to understand the man Jesus
only when she began to take yoga and her instructor introduced her
to Eastern religious thought. "I began to understand Jesus metaphys-
ically, how we have an opportunity as humans to become more like
Jesus and participate in our own health and healing process."

At one time she would have coexisted with the catch-all label
most people give such spiritual sampling. But again and again she
found the phrase *New Age* getting in the way of her efforts to articulate her beliefs. Eventually she insisted that it be dropped from the
name of the organization she founded some years ago: as a kind of
facelift, NAPRA no longer stands for New Age Publishing and Retailing
Alliance. She believes the new name, New Alternatives for Publishers,
Retailers, and Artists, helps the affiliation of publishers, stores, and
producers to avoid being pegged as fringe.

To perhaps a growing number of Americans, Marilyn McGuire's
approach holds a peculiar fascination. For some it presents an appealing alternative. Not many identify themselves as New Age, but the flavor
of that approach, the attraction of pluralism, and creating a mix-and-
match pastiche of religious influences can be tasted in wide segments
of the population. The diversity is striking.

Indeed, it would be a grave mistake to conclude that everyone in
our culture means the same thing when using the words *spiritual* or
spirituality. Americans' preferences, as we will demonstrate, reveal a
mixed bag of traditional and experimental, mainstream and fringe,
Christ-centered and syncretistic. We see in dipping from this well and

that spring a postmodern resistance to declaring one set of religious teachings true. At the very time it grows in popularity, *spirituality* has become more and more an elusive term. More and more, one crying out for definition.

> We see in dipping from this well and that spring a postmodern resistance to declaring one set of religious teachings true. At the very time it grows in popularity, spirituality has become more and more an elusive term.

Our twenty-four-hour survey helps in this. It illumines strands of a peculiarly American spirituality. Placed alongside other survey data and a broad sampling of other cultural signposts, what we learned provides an array of fascinating pictures and glimpses of what may come. What follows are our observations about the promise and pitfalls of the spiritual fascination sweeping our land.

Signpost 1: A Bull-market Spirituality

We have already begun to make the case that Americans care about spiritual issues: that strand of our corporate ethos stands out in increasingly bold relief. Those once prone to dismiss the supernatural as superstition—professors and programmers, psychiatrists and physicists—now think twice. We entertain the question, notes best-selling writer Sophy Burnham, author of *A Book of Angels:* "Are there really forces that dive, invisible, into our petty affairs?" [2] We find ourselves swept out of a compulsive reliance on the scientific method, and indeed, an insistence that everything have a method. And so the great untold story of the nineties, writes Leonard Sweet, is the global God rush. Because this seeking atmosphere affects all generations, including those that are rising, we can also say it will be the wave of a decade to come.

Certainly in our twenty-four-hour survey the answers to questions about spirituality were striking, by any reckoning. For example, we asked, "At any point during the last twenty-four hours, did you have a strong sense of God's presence?" When speaking to groups, the authors have sometimes asked audiences for guesses of the number saying yes. Most estimate ten or twenty percent. Amazingly, however,

Not only do most Americans (nine out of ten) believe in God, almost half claim to have experienced the presence of that God within a twenty-four-hour period. What is believed is also largely felt.

49 percent of our twenty-four-hour respondents recounted a sense of God's presence within the day—almost half. Not only do most Americans (nine out of ten) believe in God, almost half claim to have experienced the presence of that God within a twenty-four-hour period. What is believed is also largely felt.

The settings for these God-brushed moments vary widely, of course. For one, the sense came while holding a newborn and feeling "God's presence through that little baby." Another, struggling with illness, experienced that presence "as a healing power." A number mentioned church and times of daily prayer as the context. "God's presence is always there in whatever I do," said one respondent. One even reported a surprise encounter with a stranger: "As I was trying to sort out my thoughts, a stranger came to me and quoted a verse from the Bible: 'And my God will meet all your needs according to his glorious riches in Christ Jesus' [Philippians 4:19]. I just [bounced] right back!"

We also asked respondents if during the same period they had "a sense of being part of God's plans or purposes." Fifty-nine percent, even more than those who sensed God's presence, noted such a feeling of fitting in with something larger and grander. For an era sometimes characterized as aimless and wandering, it is striking that a strong majority made some connection of their daily lives to divine purposes. Some of the respondents elaborated with no prompting: for one, it was as simple as believing that "God has given me something to do in life." Many feel that purpose most powerfully when praying. Others conceive of a kind of cosmic game plan: if we are willing to listen to God's leading and trust what we hear, we will be led in new and surprising ways. One medical secretary who defined spirituality as "a personal relationship with Christ" said she believed that God had such a purpose for her, but admitted, "I'm not sure what that purpose is."

To no surprise, but no less significant, one of our questions confirmed striking findings from another national survey conducted in 1998: "Do you feel a need in your life," respondents were asked that year, "to experience spiritual growth?" Eighty-two percent said they felt such a need, up twenty-four percentage points in just four years. Our twenty-four-hour survey showed something similar: 78 percent said yes to the same question, roundly confirming the presence of a strong current of spiritual interest. From two surveys, then, we find that eight out of ten Americans, not just "religious" people, express desire for spiritual growth. Now, more than ever, people—including those in our pews—realize they have an ache for God. They are willing to talk about prayer in ways undreamed years ago.

Writes pastor and college professor Eugene Peterson:

> *There is a groundswell of recognition spreading through our culture that all life is at root spiritual; that everything we see is formed and sustained by what we cannot see. Those of us who grew up during the Great Spiritual Depression and who accustomed ourselves to an obscure life in the shadow of arrogant and bullying Technology can hardly believe our eyes and ears. People all around us—neighbors and strangers, rich and poor, Communists and capitalists—want to know about God. To ask questions about meaning and purpose, right and wrong, heaven and hell. . . . We may well be living during a wonderful moment in history, as those old frauds, the world, the flesh, and the Devil, are discredited by the very culture they have nearly destroyed. [3]*

Secular culture, Peterson explains, reduces all experiences, all of life, to status as "thing" and "function." People relish all the many consumables and pastimes our society makes available. But people also begin to realize that, as great as things and activities are, "getting more and doing more only makes [our] sickness worse. . . . We are surprised to find ourselves lonely behind the wheel of a BMW or bored nearly to death as we advance from one prestigious job to another." [4] That perhaps helps account for why so many now say they want to experience spiritual growth, why so many reach out for a sense of being part of a larger purpose. We realize our hunger for intimacy and transcendence. Spirituality becomes a hot topic, not simply the refuge for the dispositionally pious.

The spirituality rush does not produce of itself rich, full-orbed, and wholesome knowledge of God, of course; tingles to the spine or fleeting moments of wonder and warmth do not a life of devotion make. The interest in spirituality in itself, as we will soon show, is not an unalloyed cause for rejoicing. But it provides a starting place for conversation; it can bring life and fresh energy to stale custom; it can open people to the transforming presence of an enduringly real God.

> The interest in spirituality in itself is not an unalloyed cause for rejoicing. But it provides a starting place for conversation; it can bring life and fresh energy to stale custom; it can open people to the transforming presence of an enduringly real God.

And it promises to add life and fervor to much of our religious experience. It means a welcome retreat from an activism that assumes that goal-setting and frenzied activity and better recruitment techniques can make all the difference. The editor of *Leadership* journal, Marshall Shelley, notes how the church leaders who subscribe to his publication seem more hungry for spiritual underpinnings, not just technique. "There's less enthusiasm for church growth methods and more search for depth." The Southern Baptist Church, to give an example, launched in 1976 an emphasis called Bold Mission Thrust. The goal was to communicate the content of Christian faith to all people—worldwide—by the year 2000. At the outset of the nineties, said one Southern Baptist official, "We realized we simply were not doing it. We realized prayer was the key." Thus their new emphasis for the nineties: Bold Mission *Prayer* Thrust.

To move from broad patterns to narrative, we turn to the story of Mary Lee Bowen, a white-haired, articulate grandmother who works part-time at a Nashville luggage store when she is not talking to neighbors or volunteering at church. Her account shows spiritual renewal becoming a building force and life-altering process with wide implications for relationships.

Growing up she attended a Presbyterian church and had "a religious upbringing and strong training, especially from my mother. I never questioned that God existed." She switched to an Episcopalian congregation when she married at twenty-one. And every week of her adult life she attended the church in the county seat of Dyersburg, Tennessee, where on Sunday mornings, she said, "thirty was a big crowd." Mere attendance was not enough, however. She began to sense that something was missing.

Her sense of inner emptiness only intensified when her husband's business went bankrupt. Then her children "went wild," as she puts it; one child got involved in drugs, another was arrested for a misdemeanor. The minister at the church Bowen attended was kind, but unable to offer much spiritual sustenance or guidance. It seemed that worship had beauty and form but was, as she remembers, "dead as Hector."

Then friends invited Bowen and her husband, Gwyn, to a church in the birth pangs of charismatic renewal, a movement known for its heartfelt worship and emphasis on the Holy Spirit's activity through healing and other "signs and wonders." Bowen found the atmosphere both appealing and off-putting. "This was no-holds-barred faith," she recalls. "People you had met the week before would come up and say, 'How are you?' When you politely answered, 'Fine,' they would put a hand on your shoulder and say, 'How are you *really?*' And then once you answered more honestly they would say, 'Well, let's just pray right here in the foyer.' They had a familiarity with the Lord that took some getting used to. I found myself saying, 'How un-Episcopal!'"

Still, Bowen continued to feel drawn back. Members of the church met for prayer, Communion, and breakfast at 6:15 A.M.—every morning. "After the service we would all sit at a big table just like a family. We would have a Bible reading, a reading from [devotional writer]

Oswald Chambers, and then people would share pains and needs. We ended by standing, holding hands around the circle, and praying out loud until it was time to go at 7:30."

Her rote experience of Sunday activity began to change. Never a morning person, struggling with alcoholism, often depressed, Bowen usually found Sunday mornings a trial. But suddenly she found herself affected by the vibrancy of the congregation. "I never thought I'd see the day that I didn't want to be a minute late to Sunday School!"

One Thursday evening, while she attended a class taught by the pastor, a friend sitting to her right mentioned an experience called the "baptism in the Holy Spirit," a kind of immersion in the love and power of God, something made much of in the church. She recalls, "My friend turned to me and said, 'Well, do you want to receive it?' I said, 'Well, yes, I think I do.'" The pastor and her friend placed their hands on her shoulder and prayed for her. The experience was, as she put it, "electric": "Joy began welling up in my depths. I laughed all the way home in the car. Once home, I felt flooded with energy, even though it was 11 P.M. I told my husband, 'If I didn't think I would get arrested I would run up and down streets shouting, "I got it!"'"

Mary Lee Bowen now credits the experience with giving her a thirst for spiritual growth and Bible study. To this day, she says, her spiritual life propels her to participate in the church and to spend hours praying for others. And she credits God's grace and many church members' prayers in her children's coming to faith in God and finding a way through their struggles.

Signpost 2: A Religion of Me and Thee

Hunger for the divine sometimes places Americans, bred on the glories of self-determination and having it *my* way, in a quandary. It certainly does not always help people transcend the confines of self. It can lead to a mindset that appears individualistic and self-involved to an extreme. It fosters spiritualities that exalt the self and downplay God, that elevate our needs and whims and neglect divine mystery and sovereignty.

We found strands of this when we asked respondents to our twenty-four-hour survey to define *spirituality*. A number defined the word in sound terms like "a better relationship with God," "being in touch with God and His teachings," "enrichment through the Bible," and so on. One used clear language of biblical theology and historic creeds: "Believing that Jesus is the Son of God and the gospel that He died and on Easter morning rose with all power." But amazingly, almost a third of those in our survey defined spirituality with no reference to God or a higher authority. Here are examples:

- a calmness in my life
- something you really put your heart into
- believing in myself to make the right decisions
- having tension evolve into a whole spirit
- the essence of my personal being; each person has his or her own essence
- your relationship to people and living positively
- living the life you feel is pleasing
- the state of mind that some people have
- sensuality and one's senses; living by common sense

The answers remind the authors of a conversation reported by sociologist Robert Bellah and his cowriters of *Habits of the Heart.* Here is what one of the subjects of their study said:

> *Sheila Larson is a young nurse who has received a good deal of therapy and who describes her faith as "Sheilaism." "I believe in God. I'm not a religious fanatic. I can't remember the last time I went to church. My faith carried me a long way. It's Sheilaism. Just my own little voice. . . . It's just try to love yourself and be gentle with yourself. You know, I guess, take care of each*

*other. I think He would want us to take care of
each other.* 5

Perhaps a trend in magazine titles makes the same point: we went
from *People* magazine to *Us* to *Self,* in ever-spiraling concentric circles of inward attention. Will there soon be a magazine called *Me?* Or
a devotional periodical called *My Spiritual Self,* as though I am the
center of the process and God is a debatable option in the quest for
spiritual fulfillment? This is no mere speculation, not when writer
Patricia Hampl can argue in an introduction to a collection of spiritual essays, "It goes without saying that spiritual writing is not about
God. It is about the human longing for all that God can mean." 6

The pendulum has swung away from what is
beyond us to what is *within* us. In our twenty-
four-hour survey we asked, "Do you think of
spirituality more in a personal and individual
sense, or more in terms of organized religion
and church doctrine?" Almost three-quarters,
72 percent, opted for "personal and individual sense." Of course, the question compelled
choosing from a dichotomy that need not necessarily exist; religion at its best is *both* particular and institutional, relevant to personal
need and part of something larger. But how
striking that the weight pulls so hard on the one side. We see something similar in another question in our twenty-four-hour survey. A
clear majority (53 percent), when asked, "Do you rely more on yourself to solve the problems of life, or on an outside power, such as
God?" said they rely on self. Increasingly, it seems, people enthrone
their own wills and wants.

Said the psychiatrist to the patient, the joke goes, "I'm not clear
about your problem. Why don't you start at the beginning?"

Said the patient, "All right. In the beginning I created the heavens and the earth."

Some call this aggrandizing of self the godlet phenomenon, this modern sense that we can be gods unto ourselves, do anything, demand anything, and get anything, including adulation. No wonder we sometimes hear phrases like *guitar god* or *movie goddess* for those who have achieved a pinnacle of success and stardom. But it's not just the celebs who get the royal treatment; Madison Avenue works to tell us we deserve it all; we, too, should get what we want, when we want it. Our demands are our due.

And this tone certainly explains much of the highly publicized wariness of baby boomers to join or remain loyal to a particular denomination. They are drawn to groups and congregations that promote individual spirituality and entertain them, whatever the tag or tradition. They are less ready than previously to make a commitment or participate in congregational life. Some want nothing to do with anything that smacks of structure or doctrine. We face what someone has called an institutionalized anti-institutionalism. Much of it has to do with a penchant for the self and its interests.

At the same time, this kind of personalism, the attention to what I know and feel and reach out for, has a healthy side. The barren rationalism or cold formality of some traditions has left many in our times high and dry. They are like one woman who confessed, "All my life growing up we went to church, but that's all: we *went,* we did not necessarily pray personally or experience our faith." Surveys show that laypeople often see the church as too caught up in institutional survival or program maintenance, having lost the "spiritual" or vital part of Christian experience. Many in our nation are rediscovering, to their exhilaration, this wonderfully personal dimension. The flavor may be revivalistic or contemplative, evangelistic or high church, some theologically sound, some not. Some look for a spiritual director and take retreats at Catholic monasteries and read books by medieval mystics like Julian of Norwich, while others create missionary prayer notebooks for unreached "people groups" and organize neighborhood Bible studies. Amid great variety and theological diversity, many realize that they need not go through religious routine to obtain their deepest hungers for intimate contact with God.

Signpost 3: A Hunger for Experience

Spirituality in America sometimes appears as just one more commodity in our acquisitive, consumer drive for more. It reduces to a self-gratifying rush of soul adrenaline. Spiritual experiences can be powerful, as phenomenologist of religion William James showed almost a century ago with his seminal *Varieties of Religious Experience*. And wonderfully transforming. But now the level of expectation has risen. Someone once suggested that people no longer crave meaning in life as much as experiences. We live in an experience-saturated culture. Ads and commercials for cars and coffee and phone service no longer try to sell products; they promise ecstatic moments. And that interest carries over to faith. People come to prayer and church and Bible study expecting an experience. It is no accident that the Southern Baptists have had a phenomenon on their hands with hundreds of thousands using books and curriculum materials under the title *Experiencing God*.

Certainly respondents to our twenty-four-hour survey demonstrated an interest in experienced faith. We found that more than a third (35 percent) of our sample said there had "been a pattern in [their] spiritual life during the last twenty-four hours, with spiritual highs and lows." To elaborate, one respondent said, "I pray every day, so I am living a spiritual high." Another: "The high came when I went to corporate worship, the low last night when I should have been praying and talking with my wife; instead I was watching TV." In our earlier question asking for a definition of spirituality, many answers accented only an experienced sense of closeness: "an inner peace and connection to God," said one. In this our respondents are unwitting heirs to the late-eighteenth-century philosopher-theologian Friedrich Schleiermacher. In his shadow some today articulate spirituality in terms not formed by historic theological guidelines, but by what Schleiermacher called a "feeling of absolute dependence." Without neglecting experiential concerns, experience "has to be corrected by Scripture, the church, tradition, and objective norms," argues Beeson Divinity School dean Timothy George.

Scholar and editor Phyllis Tickle tells an illuminating story in this regard, one recorded by a colleague of hers, John Leech, an editor of a religious publishing house:

> *On vacation from seminary [in Berkeley, California] my then-wife and I drove to Arnold and walked through the groves of Calaveras Big Trees State Park. She decided she wanted to go into town and get a haircut. I tagged along. As I sat reading the waiting-bench magazines, I heard this conversation:*
>
> *—So, where are you from?*
> *—Berkeley.*
> *—Oh, I used to live there. Too many people. Why do you live in Berkeley?*
> *—My husband's in graduate school.*
> *—What's he studying?*
> *—Theology.*
> *—Theology? Huh. Never heard of it.*

"Theology," continues Tickle, is a term "far removed from the core vocabulary of current American experience." Had John's wife said he was studying religion, or especially spirituality, what a difference she could have expected in the response! [7]

Certainly, great value is inherent in a personal faith. Life-changing experiences of God's presence and love do indeed matter. One-third of Americans claim to have had a spiritual experience that touches them deeply. But much contemporary spirituality stops with experience and dispenses with reflection. It ignores or despises the larger picture that helps make sense of what we feel. In the light of some contemporary spirituality, then, it is not surprising to hear one woman describe her journey of faith as first just a "collection of peak experiences. But I had no way of linking them. I began a desperate search for a pattern."

We see this elevation of experience over belief in Neale Donald Walsch's best-selling spiritual mishmash, *Conversations with God.* He puts this bit of advice on God's lips: "Listen to your feelings. Listen to your Highest Thoughts. Listen to your experience. Whenever any one of these differ from what you've been told by your teachers, or read in your books, forget the words. Words are the least reliable purveyor of Truth." In his "conversation," Neale asks God, what about "Leaders. Ministers. Rabbis. Priests. Books. The Bible, for heaven's sake!" God's answer: "Those are not authoritative sources." [8] But what Neale and others do not realize is that emotion and personal experience take us only so far.

Other best-selling spirituality books sometimes cater to this quest for spiritual highs. The *Christian Century* recently ran a review of *Care of the Soul* author Thomas Moore's books. Reviewer L. Gregory Jones says Moore (who speaks regularly on seminary campuses) provides the reader "seductively simple ways of cultivating fantasy and keeping oneself at the center of the moral and spiritual universe." What we believe theologically is seen as irrelevant or only marginally significant. With Moore and others, instead of being pointed to "true truth" we are told to look within or "wing it." Concludes Jones, "There is a difference between responding to the wants and desires of seekers and pandering to them." The title for the review spoke volumes: "Spirituality Lite." [9] Unfortunately, the result of such approaches is anemic imitations that cannot assuage the spiritual hunger and longing for truth that God implanted in every human heart. They leave people partly gratified but still lost.

As Eugene Peterson argues in *Answering God,* "To pray by feelings is to be at the mercy of glands and weather and digestion. And there is no mercy in any of them." [10] If Satan can masquerade as an angel of light, we need more than our senses and wants and whims to find true spirituality. We need revealed truth and the steadying influence of the church. Prayer can be fed wonderfully by feeling, but cannot be based solely on it. We need an approach to spiritual experience that is grounded in tradition, saved from eccentricity (or error) through a faithful community, and kept true by recourse to God's revelation. Paul the apostle spoke of the *mind* of Christ and the importance of spiritual discernment. "For I resolved to know nothing while I was with you," he told the Corinthian church, itself infatuated with experiences, "except Jesus Christ and him crucified (1 Corinthians 2:2). There was a clear core of belief, not just experience.

Culture, then, for all its spiritual hunger, cannot in itself provide our answers. But how much do churches and religious organizations—by default and by inattention to deeply felt hungers—let popular culture provide the answers to those who are spiritually seeking? A forum held at Grace Cathedral (Episcopal) in San Francisco last year had the title, "Has Religion Left the Church Behind?" Have religious communities become so out of touch that people now seek spiritual experience elsewhere, bypassing what could and should be the one place, if any, where such can be found? When many people in our culture think about experiencing God, the church does not immediately come to mind. Research from the Barna organization found that less than a quarter of respondents say they have had an experience of God in worship services. The church even acts skittish around those who claim to have experiences of God, fearing mystical excesses.

Bible characters and "saints" through the ages were no strangers to vivid experiences of God's presence. From Moses, who sensed God in a burning bush, and later had to be hid in the cleft of a rock while the glory of God passed by; to Jesus, who knew and conversed with God intimately; to Paul, the apostle who met a risen Jesus on the Damascus road; to Julian of Norwich, a simple medieval woman who found herself plunged into a profound awareness of God's love; to Teresa of Avila, a sixteenth-century Spanish nun; to John Wesley, who told of a heart strangely warmed; to women and men of modern times, experience is not to be despised. Sometimes it overtakes us dramatically; sometimes subtly. Sometimes in a flash of revelation; more often in a dawning, building awareness. But more than many realize, people around us have regular moments of awareness of the unfathomable and ineffable.

The renewed interest in experiencing God should send us back to our heritage of spiritual resources, not make us defensive or sneering. "Ecstasy," wrote E. M. Forster, "doesn't last. But it cuts a groove for something that does last." People are waiting to be pointed to something that will endure. Ultimately, they need the intimacy with God made possible by Christ. They are ready to hear how that can happen.

This means helping people place their spiritual longings and experiences in a healthy, sound framework. Philosopher Dallas Willard points out that huge numbers of Americans claim belief in God and a personal knowledge of Jesus Christ, but seem unchanged by their experiences and beliefs. It is not that God is unable to transform, he says, but that both those on the theological right and left do not lay "down a coherent framework of knowledge and practical direction adequate to personal transformation toward the abundance and obedience emphasized in the New Testament, with a corresponding redemption of ordinary life." [11] We can be more intentional in how we form faith, encourage prayer, and invite people to a full experience of God's glory through worship and service. We do so by taking seriously the human need for experiencing God, while providing the guidelines to keep such experiences sane and wholesome.

Signpost 4:
A Search for Roots Amid the Relativism

Related to the interest in experience is our culture's alignment with postmodernism. America culture imbibes deeply from the movement, a loose philosophical stream variously (and often vaguely) defined. Among postmodernism's tenets is the assumption that truth in a final sense is unknowable. Absolute truth has instead gone the way of prescientific, tribal cultures. Inevitably, it claims, the observer contaminates the pursuit of truth through the relativity of his or her experience. What we can know must always be conditioned by the limits of our context and upbringing.

Americans, already deeply democratic in spirit, feel some attraction here. Not limiting insight or inspiration to one tradition fits into the "whatever works" mentality that has shaped our national ethos. It is no wonder that Marilyn McGuire's organization, NAPRA, has garnered interest from the publishing industry and mainstream press. The idea that one path is as meaningful as the next has shaped American religious experience profoundly. Certainly the rise of pluralism, the sheer expansion of options, has aided this. Asks a *New York Times* columnist, "At a time of growing religious pluralism in the United States, have esoteric forms of spirituality ever been so public and available?" [12]

One measure of this comes by tracing a shift in denominational affiliation. In the 1950s, sociologist Will Herberg wrote an influential book entitled *Protestant, Catholic, Jew.* Those were the primary options. But while basic religious beliefs and practices today differ little from those recorded four decades ago (nine out of ten Americans have consistently said they believe in God, seven in ten in life after death, eight in ten in some kind of Judgment Day before God), the number of people who do not fit into those groups has risen dramatically. The nation continues to become less distinctly Protestant and more pluralistic. Patterns of religious affiliation in teenagers suggest a country becoming even more pluralistic in the next generation. In 1947, only 6 percent of Americans identified themselves as anything other than Protestant, Catholic, or Jewish. In the late eighties it was 9

> In 1947, only 6 percent of Americans identified themselves as anything other than Protestant, Catholic, or Jewish. In the late eighties it was 9 percent, with the figure climbing to 19 percent among those age eighteen to twenty-four.

percent, with the figure climbing to 19 percent among those age eighteen to twenty-four.

And we see not just pluralism; the boundaries of belief within traditions seem more fluid. While only 5 percent of our twenty-four-hour respondents said they had consulted a horoscope or called a psychic hotline within the last twenty-four hours, an earlier survey suggests that 23 percent of Americans believe in astrology. Even more, well over a quarter, believe in the Eastern religious concept of reincarnation, this despite the fact that a large majority identify themselves as Christians, a faith that offers a distinctly different picture of the afterlife.

Such dipping into many wells comes partly from a new tendency to approach religion as a cafeteria lunch counter. We see more emphasis on a "salad bar" mix of this idea and that practice. Only four in ten Americans (37 percent) say they "completely agree" that there are clear guidelines about what is good or evil that apply to everyone. Relativism rules. The subtitle for a series of articles in *Utne Reader* last year illustrates the natural result: "In a mix-and-match world, why not create your own religion?"[13] And what some call "pastiche" spirituality, what one book title dubs *The Divine Deli*, seems the rage. One writer described her early faith like this: "Mine was a patchwork God, sewn together from bits of rag and ribbon, Eastern and Western, pagan and Hebrew, everything but the kitchen sink and Jesus thrown in."[14]

> One writer described her early faith like this: "Mine was a patchwork God, sewn together from bits of rag and ribbon, Eastern and Western, pagan and Hebrew, everything but the kitchen sink and Jesus thrown in."

Signs of this abound, whether in baby boomers exploring Native American shamanism; or in Sylvia Boorstein, a Jew by heritage, founding the Spirit Rock Meditation Center in California and writing a book titled *Funny, You Don't Look Buddhist;* or monasteries offering classes in yoga and Reike (healing touch). Rodger Broadley, rector of the Church of St. Luke and the Epiphany (Episcopalian) in Philadelphia, tells of several religious Jews in his congregation who come because they like the work the church does with the homeless people with AIDS. One of them wonders how in the world he can tell his parents he's going to an Episcopal church.

Wade Clark Roof, professor of religion and society at the University of California, Santa Barbara, argues that many baby boomers have assembled private faiths from bits and pieces. Some turn to new forms of more free-wheeling evangelical Christianity that appeal to "seekers" seen in megachurches such as Willow Creek Community Church, sprawling across vast acres in a Chicago suburb. Others, he notes, who turned to organized religion to give their children a context for moral training, drop out when the kids leave home for college. "It's still very much a generation whose roots in religion are very fragile, and therefore they are still open to exploring." [15]

Some have never been truly schooled in their faiths in the first place. John Berthrong, associate dean at Boston University's School of Theology, notes of his classroom, "When I talk to students about their own sense of religious identity, I find that more and more of them have been brought up in homes that are post-Christian. So to say that they are reacting against Christianity is wrong; they've never been Christians. Even some of the ones who are Christian will say, 'But I really like Taoism and Buddhism, too." [16]

Here we would argue for a recovery of theological training and biblical literacy. For churches and other religious communities of any tradition, we see the clear need to ground members more thoroughly. As we have noted, Americans are notoriously short on knowledge of basic biblical truths. "As a book," writes Wheaton College professor Gary Burge, "the Bible has been removed from the reading lists of students so that they can barely recognize metaphors from great novels written before 1950."

It is not just an issue in the wider culture, Burge notes, but even in churches, the one place where biblical literacy should flourish. He continues:

> *For the last four years, the Bible and theology*
> *department at Wheaton College in Illinois has*
> *studied the biblical and theological literacy*

of incoming freshmen. These students are intellectually ambitious and spiritually passionate. They represent almost every Protestant denomination and every state in the country. Most come from strong evangelical churches and possess a long history of personal devotion and Christian involvement. . . . They use the Bible regularly—but curiously, few know its stories. . . .[17]

These students, Burge says, very likely know that in the Old Testament story David killed Goliath, but they don't know why he did it. When asked to complete a test in which they were to put in sequence a series of biblical events (Abraham, the Old Testament prophets, the death of Christ, and Pentecost), a third could not do it. With another list of crucial biblical events, only half could put them in the correct sequence. The students simply had little sense of the millennia-long story of God's dealings with His people. [18]

We do well, then, to help people in our churches, children through adults, to learn the vocabulary of faith and the riches of our tradition. Burge tells a story that suggests why. Once he lived in an Orthodox Jewish neighborhood in Chicago. The city was rebuilding the neighborhood playgrounds. One day workers poured a small concrete retaining wall. "Later that night," recounts Burge, "when the cement was still drying, women on my street walked to the playground and wrote Hebrew sentences with carpentry nails in the cement all around the perimeter." They were verses from the Psalms, one mother told him. She said, "God's Word is powerful. Wonderful, beautiful, and I want my children to be surrounded by it while they play." [19]

Signpost 5: A Quest for Community

One of the authors was recently interviewed on the radio by a man-and-woman talk show team. The hosts were amazed that "church" and praying with others could be spoken of in the positive terms being used. For them, prayer was a matter of purely personal expression; that we might need the support and accountability of something more than personal experience seemed constricting, killing.

This rugged individualism, so pervasive in our culture, leaves millions of Americans feeling stranded. Yankelovich and associates once found that 70 percent of Americans say they have many acquaintances and few close friends, and that they experience this as a void in their lives. In our twenty-four-hour survey, we found that of all the negative feelings we asked people if they had experienced that day—guilt, fear of death, a feeling that life is meaningless—by far most who admitted such feelings singled out loneliness. Sixteen percent of our sample admitted such feelings; given that a number declined to answer the questions about their feelings at all, we can surmise the number is actually higher. Only 15 percent said they had attended a prayer service or Bible study or worship group in the last twenty-four hours. Nearly a third said that "the presence and support of others" was not important to their religious faith or personal life. They need to be gently convinced otherwise.

Americans are seeking support from a variety of sources, and to no surprise, churches not only provide opportunities for learning, worship, and spiritual nurture, they provide community. An important (by no means sole) part of that connectedness happens in small groups, whether a Sunday School class, a weekday Bible study, a twelve-step group, a singles group, a "cell group" where members worship informally and share their personal stories and receive prayer, or even a choir or other special interest grouping.

We also know that millions of Americans seek help for psychological, physical, emotional, or spiritual problems in small nurturing and caring groups, including those already mentioned, as well as book discussion clubs, sports and hobby groups, and political or civic organizations. Gallup surveys have found that 40 percent of Americans are involved in small groups that meet regularly for care, support, and nurturing, with an additional 7 percent expressing

Four in ten Americans turn to small groups for support, with another one in ten wanting to.

interest in joining such groups. Four in ten Americans turn to small groups for support, with another one in ten wanting to. The majority of participants report that they have been involved in the activity for three or more years, so we are not talking about a fad but a remarkable sociological phenomenon.

The factors that may have led—or perhaps driven—Americans to seek the solace and healing environment of small groups include:

■ *Addiction.* Recovery groups, also known as twelve-step groups, make a profound difference as people battle addictions. As a society we are addicted not only to chemicals, but to possessions, success, wealth, and a self-indulgent lifestyle, areas where small groups can provide accountability and support for new patterns.

■ *Family breakdown.* People reach out for support amid a high divorce rate, absent parents, and lack of connection to an extended family.

■ *Isolation.* We are physically detached from each other. We change places of residence frequently. One survey revealed that seven in ten do not know their neighbors. As many as one-third of Americans admit to frequent periods of loneliness, which is a key factor in the high suicide rate among the elderly.

■ *Privatism.* Americans tend to view their faith as a matter between them and God, to be aided, but not necessarily influenced, by religious institutions. The vast majority believe it is possible to be a good Christian or Jew without going to church or synagogue. A similar majority believe that people should arrive at their religious beliefs independently of any church or synagogue. Small groups can serve both as an entrance to the religious community as well as a support to those who find the church setting too impersonal.

Nearly two-thirds of all small groups have some connection to churches or synagogues. Americans' hunger for the divine lies behind at least part of their drive to join small groups and accounts for much of the pervasiveness of these groups in our culture. "This powerful movement," writes Robert Wuthnow, "is beginning to alter American society, both by changing our understandings of community and by redefining our spirituality." [20]

This is not an altogether positive current. While small groups can help people discover a deeper, warmer experience of God, they may also change the way we perceive God: they may leave us with a domesticated deity. Says Wuthnow, "The sacred becomes more personal, but in the process, also becomes more manageable, more serviceable in meeting individual needs, and more a feature of the group process itself." [21] In other words, small groups can encourage an ingrown spirituality. They need to be part of a larger community, a wider grounding in opportunities for worship, service, and outreach.

Still, they offer desperately needed help for many Americans who feel they are at the end of their emotional resources. They may want support for living a more prayer-filled life. They may want something more personal than a class or sermon or large sanctuary or synagogue. The small-group movement appears to be bringing us back together, answering what would appear to be one of the central needs of our era—for intimate and healing community.

Research also reveals the great potential of such groups for social renewal. Many participants say that as a result of participation in small groups they are more honest with themselves, better able to forgive others, more understanding of different religious perspectives, and closer to God. "What is important," notes Wuthnow, "is not just that a teenager finds friends at a prayer meeting or that a young woman finds God in Alcoholics Anonymous. These stories have to be magnified a hundred thousand times to see how pervasive they have become in our society." [22]

Surveys demonstrate that while Americans' faith is broad and pervasive, it is not always deep. As the search for meaning and intimacy seems to rise, the new spiritual curiosity may actually steer some away from formal participation in church or religious community. Not everyone will end up embracing orthodox Christian convictions, of course. But the opportunities abound for religious communities to embrace the new spiritual hunger. As they do, more and more people will experience God in the depths—and in their daily routines.

A DAY IN THE LIFE:
HOW AMERICANS TALK WITH GOD

*"How we spend our days is, of course, how we spend our
lives. What we do with this hour, and that one, is what
we are doing."*

—ANNIE DILLARD

J UST BY WATCHING him, you might not grasp how deeply
Maurice Buring cares about his religion. At any time, you are
likely to find him in motion, his wiry, agile frame striding the
aisles of his Memphis agricultural supply company set in a quiet suburban office park. When not in his office on the phone with one of
750 dealers, he's tracking inventory on his warehouse shelves—
thousands of bearings and chains for combines, cultivators, and cot-
ton pickers. It's not hard to understand how he can get absorbed in
the intricacies and stresses of a thriving business. But the fortysome-
thing man hasn't had an aspirin in the last ten years. "I believe that
comes because of what I do every Sabbath and holiday," he says.

"And by living right." His is a faith that accents on-the-job integrity, daily practices, and family ties.

It has not always been so. "A few years ago my father got very ill," he relates. "I had drifted from the practice of my faith, especially the kosher diet of Jusiasm. My dad recovered, but not before his illness made me take stock. One day I prayed, 'God, if you make him better, I will stop eating pork and will eat kosher.' I knew I needed to get back to the tradition. I've stayed with it ever since." For the past eighteen years Maurice has missed only one Sabbath or holy day service. Every Sabbath finds him leading services at the Memphis Jewish Home, a convalescent care center.

And this is no mere religion of habit and convenience. Buring's mother died recently, and now he observes the prescribed year-long mourning process. Kaddish, as it is called, has him praying twice a day for his mother, with prayers said faithfully at the synagogue every morning between 6:30 and 6:45 and at sunset. During the prescribed twelve months of observance he cannot wear new clothes; dance; or go to movies, plays, or sporting events.

His faith has a pragmatic feel, an accent on what helps him carry on with his duties. While working on his car and lifting a tire, he recalls, "My back blew out." He hit the floor, curled in pain, immobilized. He had his wife dial 911. But then he remembered that it was a high holy day and day of repentance. "'This is Yom Kippur,' I said to my wife. 'Somehow I've got to get to the convalescent home to help with the services.' She took me on her back to the shower. Somehow I managed to get ready. She drove me to the home. I made it through almost the entire service. But then I thought, *How am I going to be able to stand for the concluding part?* I did it anyway. Immediately as I stood, just like that, it happened: my back felt fine. I could go on."

Americans practice their spirituality in the small acts, daily routines, and ongoing habits, as Maurice Buring will attest. Added one by one, these little things and ordinary lives make up a family, a neighborhood or congregation or civic group, a community, a nation. The day's moments, multiplied and magnified, reveal already where we are going. How we act and pray and make decisions has inevitably set into motion circumstances and changes.

A key part of our twenty-four-hour survey explored how Americans pray in these ordinary scenes of daily life. How do they view God's relation to their activities? What ongoing prayer practices nurture them? How many respond to discouragement and despair by turning to God? How many read the Bible? We looked at American faith and practice not just during "religious" activities, but in the course of the day's business. These findings are snapshots, not sprawling canvases; vignettes more than biographies. And yet how valuable these glimpses are!

In this chapter we will focus on Americans' routines of spiritual practice, saving for the next chapter a look at how those impulses and resources manage to (and fail to) spill out into the lives of those around them.

Practice 1: Connecting Prayer and Daily Life

Americans, for all their busyness and pursuit of affluence, claim to spend considerable time reflecting on their lives. A 1998 survey showed that nearly seven out of ten respondents said they had recently thought "a lot" about "the basic meaning and purpose" of their lives, an increase from six in ten in 1985. Even more (almost three-quarters) said they thought a lot about living a "worthwhile" life. More than half had thought a lot about their "relation to God."

> The number of Americans who claim to have given "a lot" of recent thought to the meaning and value of their lives rose from six in ten in 1985 to seven in ten in 1998.

But what does that impulse to reflect look like in concrete ways? In our twenty-four-hour survey we wanted to know how Americans began their ordinary days, especially in regard to their faith. We asked, "What was the first thing you thought about this morning?"

Everyday matters abounded. One person first thought of "my baby who woke me up." One awoke wondering if he would be late for school. Another made a mental note, "Take my medication." One thought of investments that she planned "to move to another location."

A number said, "Breakfast!" or first thought groggily of "having a cup of coffee."

While it is no surprise that Americans wake up to a host of very mundane matters—commuting through traffic or dressing an irritable toddler—it is striking to see that many tie those activities explicitly to God: "I thanked God to be alive," said one. Another: "[I thought about] how hot it was, but how I was grateful to God for letting me see another day." One respondent even told us her actual waking prayer: "Lord, grant me the strength to make it through today."

Moving from the morning's first moments to the normal hours of waking life, we asked, "How, if at all, would you say your prayers related to your life during the last twenty-four hours?" A number of our respondents, not surprisingly, spoke of prayers lending a sense of "peace" or "hope" to life. They "comforted and soothed me," said one. Another asked God for "protection and His blessing." Several mentioned prayers of thanksgiving. Prayers about everyday matters continued to emerge throughout the day:

- I talk to God about everything that goes on in my life and about what goes on in the world.
- I prayed for people I knew.
- I [asked] for help for my children and my grandchildren and for all people in the world.
- We prayed for rain and we got it.
- I asked for guidance and understanding, for help in knowing how better to live my life for God.
- I was praying for food. Times have been tough and I really worry.

Fifty-five percent said that in the last twenty-four hours they had prayed at a meal, confirming other surveys that show the commonness of saying "grace" or giving thanks before (or, in Jewish custom, *after*) a meal. Meals, in other words, are frequently given a spiritual dimension, or at least a nod, in millions of American homes.

We also asked other questions about day-in, day-out experiences:

Did you "experience indescribable joy—a joy that cannot be put into words?" Nearly a third, 31 percent, said yes, suggesting what may have been fleeting moments of ecstatic awareness. "When I think about being with God," one sixty-nine-year-old Protestant pastor elaborated, "there is joy." Through the day, we asked our respondents, "Were there moments of discouragement or despair?" Fewer than a quarter (22 percent) said yes. Here, too, we get a picture of daily life feeding into prayer, and awareness of God sustaining people through routine challenges. More than half of those who faced discouragement (53 percent) said they had turned "to God or a higher power, the inner self, or Jesus Christ." This turn to divine resources may increase in our driven, fast-paced, race-to-the-top consumer culture. Tom Sine reports that 60 percent of successful professionals say that they suffer from chronic stress and depression. He also notes that the American Index of Social Health, which has tracked the well-being of Americans for twenty-five years, is fully 52 percent lower than it was in 1973, a fall that coincides with a continual rise in the gross domestic product. [1] Our abundance, which makes our daily lives materially comfortable, also distends our schedules.

How do Americans end their busy days? We asked about the last thought before going to bed the night before. Here also we found an investment in the day's activities similar to the first waking thoughts: "a fight I had just had with my fiancé," "my uncle who is in the hospital," "what I had to do the following day," and this: "I had just finished celebrating my fortieth class reunion, and was truly tired." One thought about a disturbing movie *(The Blair Witch Project)* she had just seen. Thoughts of God, or conversation with God, not surprisingly also figured significantly at the close of the day. We think of the novelist Flannery O'Connor who, after washing her face and brushing her teeth each night, would read a couple of pages of medieval theologian Thomas Aquinas, to, as she put it, "give my mind a good scrubbing." Of the fifty-four respondents who volunteered their last waking thoughts, more than a third explicitly mentioned prayer or some way of linking their day to divine purposes.

There are many ways to look at this everyday weaving in of prayer. Part of it has roots in Americans' predilection for the pragmatic, the efficient. We like to get our jobs *done,* accounting in part for our love of computers' speed and technology's ability to streamline our jobs. We think *efficiency* when it comes to prayer, too. And part of the accent on everydayness may reflect an unwillingness of Americans to extricate themselves from daily involvements long enough to ponder loftier matters. Busyness—work, taking the kids to ball practice, meetings at church—all so fill the day that no time remains for anything else, certainly not pools of quiet prayer and unhurried reflection. We are not sure we really *want* time for anything else. Writer Lee Smith put it like this: "I can't be transported. I have to go to the grocery store. I can't have a religious experience; I have to be back by three." [2] Prayer is relegated to spare moments, sometimes crowded out altogether.

But there is also something not altogether unhealthy here. Concerns of the day to come or the day behind naturally find their way into Americans' stolen moments for prayerful thought. Contrast this with times in history when believers have emphasized God's sovereignty and divine distance. They have appropriately held up a God transcending human dilemmas, accenting God's unknowability:

> *Oh, the depth of the riches of the wisdom and*
> *knowledge of God!*
> *How unsearchable his judgments,*
> *and his paths beyond tracing out!*
> *(Romans 11:33)*

And certainly the whole of Scripture, not just the Apostle Paul, speaks of a God of majesty and sovereign mystery. Still, some have taken this sense of unknowabilty too far. The deists, an eighteenth-century philosophical movement, so emphasized the inscrutability of God and the mechanical regularity of the universe that they could not imagine God involved in daily affairs. Deism does not command many formal adherents these days, but certainly many hold to a God who is just a vague presence or works only as a immanent, subtle force.

It would seem that the tide has turned, however. Many Americans imbibe Jesus' notion that God can be approached, that we appropriately pray for our "daily bread," that we can include the ins and outs of unremarkable days. We are more likely to see God as Father and Friend than Creator and Master. Ours is not a culture generally prone to otherworldly excesses. We like the concreteness of an emphasis on everyday life.

An on-line search of Amazon.com, the Internet bookseller, puts a hard number on this penchant for the world of practical and immediate concerns. Type in the word *everyday* and well-nigh 3,000 book titles using the word appear, whether *Amy Vanderbilt's Everyday Etiquette* or *The Armchair Economist: Economics and Everyday Life*. It is little different when it comes to the spiritual life:

- *Everyday Sacred: A Woman's Journey Home*
- *Being Good: Buddhist Ethics for Everyday Life*
- *The Ten Commandments: The Significance of God's Laws in Everyday Life*
- *The Art of Living Consciously: The Power of Awareness to Transform Everyday Life*
- *Beyond the Walls: Monastic Living for Everyday Life*

Such an approach seems to emphasize that God is not confined to sanctuary walls, religious custom, or sacred space. And that indeed holds promise for Americans' experience of spirituality. It reminds us that God is found in common things, in the lap of home and family, on the streets through acts of service. Americans find much help in spiritual resources for daily challenges. "Prayer is such a part of my life," said one thirty-seven-year-old artist, a Presbyterian who describes herself as "patient and particular," "that I could not live without prayers." Many also spoke of gaining strength through prayer for daily tasks.

Americans tend to find God in the midst of life, rather than the

Buddhist ideal of following the mendicant's path, living a monk's life of begging and prayer on the margins of the village. Americans emphasize a "here-and-nowness." There is something there to celebrate, and also to build on.

Psychiatrist and author Robert Coles tells how Dietrich Bonhoeffer, the martyred German theologian, would, when in the United States for a visit, go to Harlem to attend church. Not out of condescension to help the "poor," but from the conviction that Jesus was to be found among the commonest places, rather than at the seminary or the affluent churches of Manhattan. Jesus was, one could argue, present at those "religious" places as well. But Bonhoeffer realized that in the ordinariness of poverty and everyday struggle was found real Presence. The stuff of daily living has a great deal to do with faith. [3]

Practice 2: Taking Faith to Work

In light of the rediscovery of "everyday" spirituality, it is no surprise to find that Americans take this newfound sense to their workplaces. When asked, many in our survey said the first thing they thought about upon waking was work. Our survey included a paralegal, receiving clerk, banker, counselor, construction worker, electrician, an assortment of teachers and technicians, and a number of retired persons. "I prayed about the things needing to be done today," one said simply when asked about how prayer related to her day. One truck driver noted that in the last twenty-four hours he "asked God to help me get to where I have to be. And that he keep my family safe while I am on the road."

Curiously, though, not many mentioned specifically praying about the concerns of the workplace. People tend to pray about *relationships,* whether family or coworkers, as opposed to the specific challenges they face on the assembly line or sales route.

We believe that will change. For one thing, in another question, we asked, "Did you have occasion to talk about your religious faith in the workplace?" Forty-eight percent said they had—almost half!

For many, that may have been no more than a quiet, "I will be praying for you" when told of a colleague's upcoming surgery or medical test. But the answer is striking. It suggests that Americans no longer see the workplace as cordoned off from spiritual concerns.

> Americans no longer see the workplace as cordoned off from spiritual concerns. The worlds of business and religion, often compartmentalized or seen as mutually exclusive turfs, are coming together.

We also believe we are witnessing signs of new attention to work as a place for pursuing vocation, not just earning a paycheck. In a Barnes & Noble Online interview with author Po Bronson, business editor Amy Lambo asked, "Why do you write about businesspeople?" His answer reveals much about a new sense of purpose in the workplace:

> *The search for meaningful work has become an obsession over the past two decades. It is something everyone thinks about: What should I do with my life? Would I be happier doing something else? So when I write about business, even when I set my books amid money machines (like Wall Street and Silicon Valley), I write about people's struggle to find meaning in their work life. I think I would be irresponsible as a writer to ignore that this has become such a quest in our society.* [4]

There is also in our culture a new accent on seeing work as the arena for pursuing spiritual fulfillment. The corporate world plays host to new spiritual longings and experimentation with ancient truths. The worlds of business and religion, often compartmentalized or seen as mutually exclusive turfs, are coming together. "Whoever has chided commerce for being utterly secularized," writes Martin Marty, "has to take notice and do some reappraising." Marty cites *U.S. News & World Report* (May 3, 1999) that featured the topic in a story by Marci McDonald. "Spirituality is the latest corporate buzzword," reads the tagline of the article, "Shush. The Guy in the Cubicle Is Meditating." [5] Tom Chappell's *Soul of a Business* became a hot book commodity. One of the best-selling business books of all time, *The 7 Habits of Highly Effective People,* is laced with philosophical and spiritual wisdom. "Some of the more open-minded CEOs we know," says corporate consultant and "trend guru" Faith Popcorn, "are consulting with spiritual guides to help them understand their business." [6] Advocates for bringing prayer and spirituality into the workplace point to pragmatic benefits such as increased morale and productivity. "Expect both praise and criticism to grow," notes Marty, "as 'spirituality' increasingly finds its home in management seminars and corporate policy and practice." [7]

Indeed, there are pluses and minuses, issues to be resolved in the forging of new connections between faith and the workplace. Many business executives argue that spirituality, allegedly vague and noncreedal, is not to be confused with religion. Yet while promotion of a particular religion is usually frowned upon, some of the meditation techniques advocated in some employee training programs import explicit categories from Eastern religions. And one might wonder, Will some employees take advantage of the new openness to browbeat colleagues? No doubt. But laws and common sense usually ensure that no employees feel pressured by unwelcome buttonholing or religious nagging.

People also seem bent on carrying their faith into the workplace in more than quiet or surreptitious ways. Groups that meet for spiritual nurture or religious instruction *on the job site* are flourishing, as noted in this *New York Times* article:

> *It is Wednesday, and Louis Tuchman's appointment book is packed, as usual. At 9:45 A.M., he huddles with a fellow lawyer to fine-tune two major real estate deals. At noon, he skips lunch to return phone calls and sign documents. But at 12:30 P.M., Mr. Tuchman steps*

into his firm's boardroom on the 14th floor of the Chrysler Building for what he calls the most important meeting of all.

The weekly Torah class.

Mr. Tuchman is part of a wave of thousands of professionals who, pressed for time and afraid they have neglected their faith, are organizing religion classes in hundreds of companies across the nation. From Bible study lunches at Northrop Grumman to noon Torah classes at Microsoft and Islamic study groups at Intel, these classes are proliferating at what religious scholars say is a breathtaking pace.

"People are rediscovering religion in their own terms," said Max L. Stackhouse, professor of Christian ethics at Princeton Theological Seminary. "This is happening all over the place, and it's increasing like mad. . . ."

In all, there is a sense that people are not only embracing religion in different ways, but also have become more comfortable in the public expression of their faith. With that, the barriers separating work and religion are crumbling. [8]

More and more people are realizing that prayer and work need not be separate domains.

Ideally, the new spiritual interest in work and prayer should be ultimately a positive influence. Robert Coles tells of a man working on an assembly line at a General Electric factory in Massachusetts: "I won't tell you I'm in heaven when I'm there on the [assembly] line." And yet his work is not purely secular occupation, but also one into which he weaves themes of the sacred:

I show up [on the job] early and leave late. I clock in the hours—and I bring home the bacon: that's life. Sundays, in church, I'll hear about all the troubles that came His way, to Jesus, and I say to myself: hey mister, He was the Son of God, that's what He was, and look at all that happened to Him. Can you imagine, being nailed up like that, and no one giving a hoot or a holler about you. . . . The lesson: don't feel sorry for yourself! Don't slack off in self-pity. . . . So, [while I'm on the job], I think of the sermon or one of the hymns, and I try to keep on my toes. [I try] to live as Jesus did, at least some of the time. [9]

Practice 3: Taking Prayer to Heart

We found it remarkable that more than two-thirds of our respondents said they had prayed within the last twenty-four hours. In a way, though, that is not surprising: Surveys have for decades shown that nine in ten Americans say they pray. Others suggest that 75 percent "pray daily." Nearly all who pray believe their prayers are heard and have been answered. A majority of 55 percent of those who pray say that, compared to five years ago, prayer is now more important to them. No wonder a *Newsweek* cover story on prayer some years ago declared, "This week, if you believe at all in opinion surveys, more of us will pray than will go to work, or exercise, or have sexual relations." [10] Americans appear to gravitate toward the topic, not perhaps to the extent they did with angels in the early nineties, not with quite the same infatuation, but nevertheless in real ways. They do not always feel particularly *competent,* but they certainly feel drawn. Even people who do not typically practice their faith actively will say to a friend in distress, "I will pray for you."

We also asked our respondents, "Do you recall what you prayed

> A majority of 55 percent of those who pray say that, compared to five years ago, prayer is now more important to them.

for or about?" "I prayed for a host of things," said one, "nothing particularly stands out in my mind." But more generally respondents could remember, and their answers ranged far and wide. There were, for example, many prayers about family:

- I prayed for a blessing for my son, that he will be a good person.
- I prayed to be happy and to have a healthy family.
- I prayed for help for my mother and guidance for myself.

This confirms the 1993 *Life* magazine/Gallup survey in which 98 percent of the respondents, the largest group of all, said they had at some time prayed for their "family's well-being."

At 94 percent, "giving of thanks" was the second largest category in the *Life*/Gallup survey. And we found gratitude for things large and small in our twenty-four-hour survey: prayers of thanks ranged from "I thanked God for what we have and for families around the world," to "I thanked God for waking me so early this morning."

There were ample prayers for guidance, the third most common category—prayers, for example, "that God would change my life and that I would be able to live it for Him" and "for guidance that I make the right decisions." As with the other top categories, nine out of ten Americans say they have prayed such prayers for guidance.

We also found prayers for forgiveness, for peace in the world, for people caught in violent crossfire, and many prayers of petition for family members and daily needs. Americans pray for missionaries carrying the Christian message around the world and for hurting neighbors next door. They pray to find lost keys and pray to reach out to lost souls.

Given the stereotype of prayer being nothing more than seeking selfish gain, we found another fascinating fact in the *Life*/Gallup survey born out in our twenty-four-hour survey. Only 23 percent in that 1993 survey said they had prayed for victory in an athletic event, while even fewer, 18 percent, said they prayed for material things such as winning the lottery or getting a raise or new car. In a similar way, we found that while some prayed for "daily needs," the bulk of requests seemed remarkably shorn of materialism. Were people simply not volunteering or choosing to forget requests bathed in acquisitiveness? Perhaps. But that so many of our respondents said they prayed about weightier matters, or prayed for other people, or sought forgiveness for wrongs that still pained them, hints at a healthy recognition that prayer should at least at times go beyond mere asking for things.

And indeed, Americans seem to sense that contrition, petition, and intercession all belong in a healthy growing prayer life, as do silence and moments of simple communion with God. However, amid all the requests and confessions, that note of simply sitting in the presence of Ultimate Love did not always come through in respondents' answers. No one specifically mentioned praising God for who He is. We come into God's presence, our oldest spiritual mentors and wisest teachers tell us, through invitations *both* to "ask . . . seek . . . knock" as well as to "be still and know that I am God."

> We asked, "Do you sometimes feel that modern life leaves you too busy to enjoy God or pray as you would like?" Not surprisingly, more than half (51 percent) said that was the case.

What about time to pray? We asked, "Do you sometimes feel that modern life leaves you too busy to enjoy God or pray as you would like?" Not surprisingly, more than half (51 percent) said that was the case. Nevertheless, the same percentage in the 1993 *Life*/Gallup survey said that at home they "always" or "frequently" said grace (gave thanks) for meals. Only 14 percent say they never do. Furthermore, 3 percent said they are "constantly in a state of prayer." Apparently some feel able to heed the injunction of the Apostle Paul to "pray without ceasing."

How prayer and spirituality dovetail with our sometimes harried life seems to be more and more a topic of concern for Americans. In 1999, *The New York Times* ran a story titled "Squeezing in Soul Time; New Yorkers Take Five from the Workday to Feed the Spirit." The article described the prayer practice of Rick Hamlin, an editor for the interdenominational magazine *Guideposts* (and author of *Finding God on the A Train*). While Hamlin attends church and other corporate prayer experiences, his personal prayer time often occurs on the commuter train he takes every weekday. "I don't clock myself, but I use the subway stops as markers, guiding me in my ritual. I read from the 181st Street station, usually from the Bible, occasionally from what my wife calls a 'God book,'—a work by some metaphysical sage, recent or not so recent." [11] Then, when his train rolls out of the 125th Street station in Harlem and glides on express tracks toward midtown, he concentrates on prayer. "I'm almost ashamed to admit how short it is," said Hamlin. "It just doesn't sound like very much time, but there's a lot you can accomplish in that time." The article continued:

> *These days, scholars of religion say, urban dwellers are increasingly seeking ways to squeeze spiritual and religious observances into moments that crop up during busy workdays, even as interest in organized religion wanes.*

"A lot of people have the sense that spirituality is nurtured in stolen moments during the day," says Randall Balmer, a professor of religion at Barnard College and Columbia University. "It may be a coffee break or between phone calls or at lunch hour. It is a testimony to the highly individualistic state of religion today, although 'spirituality' is a better word to describe it." [12]

Practice 4: Returning to Tradition

Some Americans are waking up to concerns about the "highly individualistic state of religion" that Balmer spoke of. Despite the "salad bar" spirituality and experimentation we talked about in the last chapter, there is a countercurrent: to draw from the ancient and time-tested, to uncover older, communal sources for spiritual nurture. Tradition, sometimes seen as constricting, now more frequently appears in an appealing light. Churches, with a heritage of thousands of years of insight and witness and worship, can take heart.

It is no accident, for example, that one can find nearly forty thousand titles in print containing the words *classic* or *classics.* "Retro," a look or feel reminiscent of older times, is no longer musty, but hip. We need not assume in our culture that "old" will always be a turn-off or tune-out. It may hold peculiar fascination for those nonplussed by an overload of experimentalism.

> We need not assume in our culture that "old" will always be a turn-off or tune-out. It may hold peculiar fascination for those nonplussed by an overload of experimentalism.

In the specifically religious milieu as well, tradition, once despised as an encumbrance, may be in for a return. A number of Christian publishers have launched series of spiritual classics: *The Classics of Western Devotion, The Upper Room Spiritual Classics, Rekindling the Fire.* Kathleen Norris provides another striking example of the search for ancient roots. The phenomenally popular poet and essayist used to believe monasteries were the stuff of medieval lore. Then she found herself, a Presbyterian and still married, drawn to live nine months at St. John's Abbey in Minnesota. Her 1996 book, *The Cloister Walk,* chronicling her time there, stayed on the national best-seller lists for twenty-seven weeks. Who would have thought that a journal of a monastic sojourn would capture best-seller status and spawn numerous spin-offs?

Other signs of a reclamation of the traditional roots of spiritual life:

■ Conservative Christian groups continue to grow while more "desacralized" or nontraditional denominations decline. Based on an average of two Gallup surveys conducted in 1997, more than four in ten Americans (44 percent) described themselves as born-again or evangelical Christians, the highest figure recorded to date, only to be topped again in 1998 with 47 percent. The latter represents an eleven-point increase since 1994, when the figure was 36 percent. (In certain Gallup surveys, a tighter definition based on a three-part index has been used, in which case the number drops to one person in five. The three parts: (1) have a born-again experience, (2) believe the Bible is the literal or actual word of God, (3) have tried to encourage someone to accept Jesus Christ as his or her Savior.) And of course, basic belief in God is as high as it has ever been in recent memory. In our twenty-four-hour survey, 79 percent affirmed, "I know God really exists and I have no doubts about it."

■ Once eager to throw out chant and Latin phrases and ancient liturgy, many Catholics now see a kind of "retro revolt" taking place. *Time* magazine recently featured an article about Catholics, including some Gen-Xers, who demand recovery of Latin in the mass. The reforming, modernizing spirit of Vatican II and the general liberalizing trends of the 1960s leave some hungry for the liturgical customs once discarded as archaic. At thirty-two, Catherine Muskett is one of those asking for tradition. "To her," reports *Time,* "today's perky folk-guitar Masses are more grating than groovy. 'Catholics of my generation are starved for the real thing,' she says. So each Sunday, she and her family drive half an hour to attend the Solemn High Mass, most of it in Latin, offered by St. Catherine of Siena Catholic Church in Great Falls, Virginia. Like some catacombed underground movement, they take out old Gregorian missals for translation and sing Palestrina instead of Peter, Paul and Mary. . . . Since 1990, the number of U.S. Catholic dioceses allowing traditional Masses (in Latin or a mix of English and Latin) has leaped from six to 131—70 percent of the total. More than 150,000 people attend them each week." 13

■ On the same page, *Time* reported on Reform Jews deciding to reclaim the skullcap (yarmulke), abandoned in earlier decades for lack of relevance. "They have been debating, avidly, for two years, and when their leaders gathered in Pittsburgh, Pennsylvania, to settle the matter, discussion dragged on for an unscheduled half a day. But at noon last Wednesday, the domed sanctuary of Pittsburgh's historic Rodef Shalom Congregation rang with cheers. By a vote of 324 to 68, the leadership of the 1.5 million-member Reform movement, the most liberal of American Judaism's three big branches, accepted the inevitability of the yarmulke." While that may be a bit of oversimplification, the article continued, "at major Reform gatherings, half the heads are covered; congregants hunger for once discarded traditionalism. Says Rabbi Paul Menitoff of the Central Conference of American Rabbis, who shepherded last week's new Statement of Principles: 'Our grandparents' challenge was to become acculturated. Our challenge is to be more in touch with our roots.'" [14]

■ With even more relevance for what the next decade and century hold, teens demonstrate a return to roots in their religious faith. In a 1998 Gallup survey reported by the Associated Press, nearly all teens (92 percent) consider their religious beliefs important to them. Nearly nine out of ten say they believe in the divinity of Jesus. A majority of teenagers read the Bible at least monthly. When scientific explanations and religioius explanations conflict, a strong majority (62 percent) say they prefer religious explanations. The latter finding has fascinating implications on a number of levels. Mixed in with it is doubtless a fascination with the paranormal and darkly supernatural. But it may also suggest a larger dissatisfaction with a rigid scientism. It may leave room for belief in intelligent design, which is not a simplistic antievolutionism, but belief that from the smallest to the greatest units of existence, the hand of a Creator is evident. [15]

We also see at least traces of traditional devotion when we note how many American adults read the Bible and turn to it for guidance and solace. A 1998 Gallup audit of Bible reading found that 38 percent said they read the Bible weekly or more often. The number in our twenty-four-hour survey who claimed to have read the Bible in the last twenty-four hours is similar: 36 percent. This compares with 5 percent who said they had read their horoscope or called a psychic hotline in the same period. Despite the bad news about biblical literacy in our last chapter, Americans don't seem to completely neglect the Bible. We will say more later about the key role the Bible must have in grounding devotional life—and all life—in revealed truth, but for now we note that the Bible, sometimes called "the greatest story never read," does gain some hearing in American homes.

We also see a concern for form and tradition in the nature of Americans' actual prayers. While one of our respondents described his prayers as for "whatever comes to mind," many find that is not enough. An impulse to move beyond a diet of freelanced prayers leads some to pray with others or to delve into classics of devotion. Left to ourselves, our prayers tend to major only on those people right next to us; they can and should be so much more. Fortunately we see new awareness that all that feeds faith does not come from within or on the spot.

> While one of our respondents described his prayers as for "whatever comes to mind," many find that is not enough. An impulse to move beyond a diet of freelanced prayers leads some to pray with others or to delve into classics of devotion.

Indeed, when most American adults pray, they usually turn to a Supreme Being such as God, the Lord, or Jesus Christ. According to a Gallup survey conducted in late 1993 for *Life* magazine, very few pray to a mere force or New Age "God within." Americans prefer traditional terms of address for God:

To whom or to what do you pray most often?

- ■ *A supreme being such as God* — *75%*
- ■ *Jesus Christ* — *16%*
- ■ *The Lord* — *3%*
- ■ *Jehovah* — *1%*
- ■ *A transcendent or cosmic force* — *1%*
- ■ *To my inner self/the God within* — *1%*

The content of prayer also warrants comment. The *Life*/Gallup survey showed this breakdown of types:

- ■ *Conversational* — *56%*
- ■ *Meditative or reflective* — *15%*
- ■ *Formal, such as the* — *13%*
  Lord's Prayer/Our Father
- ■ *Combination of all three* — *14%*

Protestants are twice as likely as Catholics to say they engage in conversational prayer (65 percent to 31 percent). Catholics far more often than Protestants say their prayers are more formal expressions such as the Lord's Prayer.

This disparity, we predict, will narrow. Catholics seem more and more to imbibe from an evangelical spontaneity in matters of devotion. Protestants find themselves drawn to liturgy and classical writings of devotion. There seems to be a new fascination with the past for both Catholics and Protestants (and Orthodox and independent). Across the denominational board, people rediscover that the old can have fresh relevance, whether from the Protestant heritage in Martin Luther, John Calvin, John Bunyan, John Wesley, Jonathan Edwards, Charles Spurgeon, and C. S. Lewis, or from the Catholic heritage in Augustine, John Chrysostom, Benedict, Francis, Julian of Norwich, Thomas à Kempis, Brother Lawrence, John of the Cross, Teresa of Avila, and Thomas Merton. One man puts his rediscovery of the riches of tradition like this: "I feel that my connection to the Church is based on the full two thousand years of tradition and testimony. Now when I peruse Christian bookstores, I no longer feel pressured to keep up with the latest additions to the publishing market; I have plenty of time-tested teachers to read—and re-read."

Will there continue to be such cross-fertilization? A rigid return to tradition can make groups buttress themselves against others' insights and heritage. David Bryant of Concerts of Prayer, International, and the National Prayer Committee uses a hopeful analogy, however. He sees what is happening amid the varied Christian traditions and approaches as "pools of renewal." "The spiritual formation people who emphasize a more contemplative approach are digging deeper," he says. "Someone who emphasizes intercessory prayer for the nation digs wider, and we're all saying something is going on out there of tremendous spiritual significance, that we have never seen before. The Lord wants to get our 'pools' flowing together."

Certainly there are signs of this. Richard Foster, a widely known Quaker writer on spiritual disciplines, founded some years ago an organization called Renovaré (the name is based on a Latin root that means "renew"). This nondenominational group, with its publications and network of small spiritual formation groups, lays out a vision of the church that draws on all its streams, ancient and modern: contemplative, holiness, charismatic, social justice, evangelical, and incarnational. [16] There seems to be a growing interest in an approach to the spiritual life not given to fads or limited to narrow visions.

Of course, those of us in the Christian tradition have a challenge. Ours is not the only ancient tradition being rediscovered. In their rediscovery of spirituality many may turn to any number of options in an ever-spreading spiritual smorgasbord. They may even become mired in deception. Many in our postmodern culture see Eastern practices and esoteric worldviews as the epitome of depth and transforming power, while they ignore the wealth of Christian devotion—the centuries of powerful encounter with God, of profound exploration of spiritual reality. Notes Episcopal priest and author Richard Kew, "There is within the Christian tradition a richness in both spiritual exercises and disciplines of meditation that far exceeds anything found in the Eastern religions." [17] Will Americans realize that or assume that other traditions hold the key to what they long for?

> Christianity is not the only ancient tradition being rediscovered. In their rediscovery of spirituality many may turn to any number of options in an ever-spreading spiritual smorgasbord.

Where Prayer Will Take Us

One retired Baptist respondent on the twenty-four-hour survey described her prayers like this: "[I prayed] for my family, friends, the sick and shut-in, missionaries throughout the world, all the little children—that He would save the lost ones, and then I thanked God for my life, health, and strength."

How will God use such prayers? Who can begin to know or answer? Prayer and spiritual fervor do not put strings on a sovereign God. The fruit of an increase of prayer may not always be visible.

Indeed, says Robert Mulholland of Asbury Theological Seminary in Kentucky, "we may well be entering a time of the sifting of the church." Through that, God may be bringing a faithful remnant "into deeper levels of discipleship that will enable them to endure" in a culture that for all its spirituality seems to become post- or even anti-Christian.

It is a sign of hope that Americans continue to ensure that they pray, whether on the job, like Maurice Buring, or in services or set "quiet times." But there is room for growth. Focusing on everyday spirituality may become a way of managing God, confining Him to passing glances or blurted snatches of conversation. Paradoxically, this approach may also explain in part Americans' fascination with the supernatural, with spiritual experiences, with angels and healings and channeling. Such dramatic encounters allow people to point to one or two or a few remarkable, mysterious experiences, surmises Robert Wuthnow. Precisely because they are exceptional, people can nurse the remembrance of such rare occurences, living off them and neglecting to go deeper. Because such interventions have an aura of mystery, we can tell ourselves they are past understanding and need not take much of our time. We content ourselves with the exceptional epiphany. "The spiritual realm," concludes Wuthnow, "is thus a reality that people can muse about in everyday life, but its location remains on the periphery of their daily routines. It diverts little of their attention." [18]

And yet if more Americans are praying more, there is reason for hope. Those who have studied the nation's religious revivals argue that such renewal has always been preceded by an increase of prayer. Jonathan Edwards, encouraged by the outbreak of lively prayer societies spreading across Scotland (and soon to spread across the American colonies), wrote in 1748 that Christians should "pray to God in an extraordinary manner, that he would . . . pour out his Spirit, revive his work, and advance his spiritual kingdom." Through such praying, he continued, "at length will gradually be introduced a revival of religion."

Will today's recovery of prayer, at least its healthier side, lead to some similarly profound renewal of our corporate life and an awakening of our sleeping-giant churches? And will an increasing number of transformed lives spill over into our life as a nation as a whole? The Bible affirms that wholesome prayer will not escape God's notice. If we are praying for our friends, our churches, our communities, our lost and lonely and poor, who knows how God may answer—and lead us to become part of the answer? We will have more to say about the possibilities of that later.

A DAY IN THE LIFE: HOW AMERICANS NEED AND HELP OTHERS

"A candle loses nothing by lighting another candle."
—PROVERB

"God does not so much need people to do extraordinary things as he needs people who do ordinary things extraordinarily well."
—WILLIAM BARCLAY

IT WAS THE people huddled in cars on a December night in 1985 that changed Charles Strobel's life. The six-foot-tall Catholic priest, slight, beginning to bald, with a touch of gray in his brown hair, recalls that first scene:

> *As I looked out my bedroom window from the rectory beside the church, I saw a disturbing*

*scene. People were asleep in their cars parked in
the church parking lot, and the temperature that
evening was dropping below freezing.*

*I felt compelled to do something. I went
down and invited everyone to spend the night
in the cafeteria.*

*I didn't think too long about it, probably
because I knew I would talk myself out of it. . . . I
knew that the consequences were far greater than
simply giving a dozen men one night's lodging.
What do you do about tomorrow night and on
and on? . . . What would my parishioners say? For
the moment I decided it was the only thing to do.*

The Rev. Strobel's hunches proved true: what he was about to do
would have lasting consequences. He invited the people to stay the
night, he says, "and they stayed the winter."

Soon a friend from the Salvation Army arranged for cots, blankets,
and some staff assistance. A number of church groups brought in food
in the evenings, and Strobel's own parishioners got more involved
(some were already involved in a community meal program). By the
time spring rolled around, the group gathered enough momentum to
run a shelter year-round. They found a site, and Matthew 25, the name
for the new enterprise, became one of Nashville's most successful per-
manent shelters for the homeless. But sheltering forty working men
was not enough; the needs were far greater.

Late in 1986, Strobel and his associates realized they needed more
partners. They launched Room in the Inn, an interfaith effort of churches and synagogues of every stripe. Eventually he led 145 churches in
Nashville to open their doors to provide food and shelter on a rotating
basis for 200 homeless people each night during the winter months. In
1998 alone, volunteers gave more than 100,000 hours of their time.

The burgeoning work led Strobel to trade his parish duties for
full-time work with a ministry agency called The Campus for Human

Development. It means multiplied programs to help people in need, partnering with many, including the Nashville Metro Health Department. The Campus occupies a two-story, 10,000-square-foot warehouse in downtown Nashville, just like all the drab warehouses that dot the urban landscape. But much more happens there than in the typical factory or storage building. The facility is the hub for Room in the Inn. The Guest House program provides an alternative to jail for fifteen to twenty-five intoxicated people picked up each day by the police. The Day Center provides emergency services, showers, and rehabilitation programs. Educational programs help with life skills, career education, health education, and GED classes.

What was it about that winter's night in 1985 that so changed Strobel's ministry? "It made a difference that the homeless people were right before me," reflects Strobel. "There were others down the street, on the riverbanks, in the vacated buildings, or hovering over the sidewalk grates, but I couldn't see them. Somehow, it's different when they aren't right before us. Maybe it's easier to think they're someone else's problem. But that night these people were no one's problem but mine. So I invited them to spend the night."

While more dramatic than most, Strobel's experience of awakening to the needs of others takes place countless times across our country. Of course, we do live in times, as we have seen, when many people elevate the self to supreme status. Many experience the effects of what one television program called "Affluenza," the soul-deadening malaise of materialism. The gap between the haves and have-nots widens. The wealthiest 1 percent of households in America, says George Barna, owns more than 40 percent of the nation's assets. Forty percent of America's poor are children. "Despite these glaringly apparent needs," notes Barna, "churches across the country are minimally involved in addressing this issue. For every dollar spent on ministry to the poor, the typical church spends more than five dollars on building and maintenance." [1]

But Americans also heed another impulse, one with roots deep in the Judeo-Christian heritage, one that makes compassion for neighbor both an ideal and a sometime reality. And while this impulse to help and offer spiritual insight leads to individual acts of compassion and witness, Americans sense that solo efforts will go only so far. They know that the nation's social problems must also be addressed corporately.

Fortunately, our churches and religious institutions are in place to leave a more profound imprint on society. Deep in the Christian message lies the conviction that devotion finds its expression in more than praise to God but also in service and proclamation to others. In the New Testament we read of a Jesus who went about doing good (Acts 10:38). Commented one writer, "Why are we content with merely going about?"

> Deep in the Christian message lies the conviction that devotion finds its expression in more than praise to God but also in service and proclamation to others.

Churches can do much to help people help people. The benefits of friendship and fellowship do more than make believers feel good inside—they can enable reaching out to those in physical and spiritual need. The journey inward, to echo Elizabeth O'Connor's phrase, can equip the next millennium's church for an renewed journey outward. Already the signs are in place that millions of Americans are not content with prayers of "Bless us four and no more." In soup kitchens and homeless shelters and crisis pregnancy centers and classrooms and employee lunchrooms, at dining room tables and church halls, spiritual life spills over into the lives of others. To keep that happening in the coming decade will require strengthening the ties that bind us together, the ties that ultimately motivate us to go out from the temple or sanctuary's four walls.

The Faith Factor

Cynics would say that spiritual experiences so absorb the soul in otherworldly pursuits that it becomes oblivious to others. The idea is that spirituality numbs us to others' pain. And such a scenario is possible;

some find in cozy spiritual groups a refuge from the needs that beset our cities and schools and government. Religion becomes a tranquilizer. It soothes the already comfortable, assuring them that if God is "in control," they need not trouble over the needy. Me-centered faith becomes, as we have seen, a compulsive quest for charged moments that ultimately neither fulfill nor transform, that carry no benefit to another.

Americans certainly give religion mixed marks on this score. In 1996, a strong majority (57 percent) said they felt religion was "losing its influence on America." Even more (68 percent) said so in 1994. While the question did not parse all the elements of that influence, surely part of it was a sense that the church should have greater impact on the day's great social needs—poverty, violence, disregard for the sanctity of life. Religion's institutions sometimes seem to get in the way of the call to love our neighbor and clothe and feed the poor, in the tradition of Jesus' Parable of the Good Samaritan. Some pastors and church leaders worry that emphasizing spiritual growth will leave their people passive, anesthetized to a lost and hurting world.

Research shows, however, that people often turn to others in need out of religious motivations. Wholesome spirituality does not hinder that outward turn, but fortifies it. Jesus, after all, linked the Great Commandment both to loving God with heart, mind, soul, and strength and loving one's neighbor as one's own self.

The data gives empirical weight to Jesus' linking. It is no accident that in our highly churched nation, one American in every two gives two or three hours of effort each week to a volunteer cause. This "volunteerism" often has behind it a church or other religious group. Historically, synagogues and churches have catalyzed or founded hospitals, nursing homes, universities, public schools, and child-care programs. And today many take meals to shut-ins, lead a Boy Scout troop, or volunteer for soup kitchens through the auspices and with the encouragement of a congregation. A Gallup survey conducted for Independent Sector revealed that America's religious institutions practice what they preach. Religious groups are major sources for volunteer services for our neighborhoods and communities. Indeed, probably no other institution in our society has had a greater impact for good than the church. We see, for example that:

- Almost half of the members of a church or synagogue did unpaid work in a given year, compared to only a third of nonmembers.
- Nine in ten (92 percent) members gave money to a charity, compared to only seven in ten (71 percent) of nonmembers.
- Eight in ten members (78 percent) gave goods, clothing, or other property to a charitable organization, compared to two-thirds (66 percent) of nonmembers.
- Eight in ten report that their religious beliefs help them to respect and assist other people.

In our book *The Saints Among Us*, we uncovered a similar pattern. We found a representative sample of America's everyday saints through a survey with twelve questions describing spiritual commitment and attitudes toward prayer, doctrine, and evangelism. We determined that this core of "highly spiritually committed" make up 13 percent of the population. (Would that they made up more!) These "hidden holy" not only seemed exceptional in their faith, they excelled in compassion. Seventy-three percent of these "ordinary" believers claimed to spend a good deal of time helping the needy; whereas, with those we termed the strongly *un*committed, the percentage dropped to 42 percent. That was just one of several differences we noted between the saints and the general population; we found markedly lower amounts of racial prejudice among the highly spiritually committed, to cite another. And a number of the saints told of specific people they had helped, concrete acts that made a world of difference; one had just given baby items to a young Korean mother new to the United States. Others helped victims of cancer, visited and prayed with the hospitalized, volunteered in church programs, and gave money to charities. Little things, all, but powerful in their accumulating effect. Their faith played a significant part. [2] With all the new millennium's momentous stresses and tears to the fabric of society, the church must not neglect the potential of acts of service to hold society together. And churches have power not only to facilitate acts of kindness, they can lend their weight to social policies that guard the dignity of neighbors, the sacredness of life. Many will volunteer for concrete acts. Others will be called to an activism that changes the root causes, as well. Both are vital.

> With all the new millennium's momentous stresses and tears to the fabric of society, the church must not neglect the potential of acts of service to hold society together.

Our twenty-four-hour survey confirmed this faith-compassion connection. "During the last twenty-four hours," we asked, "was there an occasion when you went out of your way to help someone else because of spiritual or faith reasons?" Not quite half (45 percent) said yes. Some acts were simple to the extreme: "I helped a boy across the street." One helped a colleague at work. A fifty-one-year-old principal visited residents in a nursing home to "reach out" to others.

> Forty-five percent said they went out of their way to help someone in need because of spiritual or faith reasons during the last twenty-four hours.

Sometimes, of course, the cost of helping is very great. It requires more than an odd hour or two volunteered in convenience. In September 1999, a woman at Wedgwood Baptist Church in Fort Worth, Texas, scene of a much-publicized Wednesday evening shooting at a youth rally and worship service, placed her body between the gunman and a special-needs child named Heather. The woman, Mary Beth, sustained a bullet wound in the back. She will recover, but she modeled costly compassion. Her example of sacrificial love echoed around the world. Some forego comfort by living in dangerous neighborhoods, receiving less pay for socially beneficial jobs, or making themselves available for suicide hot lines at awkward times of the day or night. Some, like Charles Strobel, find themselves called to a life work of helping the needy. Many more offer their work as teachers, accountants, lawyers, social workers, and nurses as not just professions, but *helping* professions. And whatever the job, millions of Americans give at least occasional reflection to seeing their workplace as a place to share faith and show compassion.

Such involvements no doubt strengthen those in our survey who, when asked, said they had a sense of "being part of God's plans or purposes" in the last twenty-four hours. A strong majority of 59 percent said they had had a sense of "being part of God's plans or purposes." Being of help to others becomes a way to live out the prayer that "God's will be done on earth, as it is in heaven." Further, when we asked, "Do you believe you have gifts or abilities from God?" 79 percent said yes. More than three-quarters, then, believe their talents are more than possessions to be used only for personal gain. No doubt this conviction was born in the saddle of actual service. We asked, for instance, "Did you have a chance to use these gifts or abilities during the last twenty-four hours?" A clear majority (58 percent) said yes.

Sociologist Robert Wuthnow also confirms the power of the "faith factor" in the web of compassion that crisscrosses our national life. Wuthnow argues that spiritual practice and service indeed are "interlaced." Religious faith energizes service. Among the people he interviewed, he notes, "spending time cultivating their relationship with God seemed more often to free them from material concerns and other self-interested pursuits so they could focus on the needs of others." [3] Spirituality and social action, in other words, so often pitted as an either/or, really can be a both/and.

The monk and spiritual writer Thomas Merton made a similar point. It is the weak soul, he says, echoing Bernard of Clairvaux, that arrives at deep prayer "but does not overflow with a love that must communicate what it knows to other [people.]" For all the great saints, Merton stresses, "the peak of the mystical life is a marriage of the soul with God which gives the saints a miraculous power, a smooth and tireless energy in working for God and for souls, which bears fruits in the sanctity of thousands and changes the course of religious and even secular history." [4] A profound experience of divine love, in other words, leaves us with love to spare, with an overflowing power to share what we have with those who do not.

But this connection of faith and works is not automatic. From research for his book *Acts of Compassion,* Robert Wuthnow notes that church and synagogue play a much larger role than once thought in keeping faith from stagnating into self-centered spiritual pursuits. Usually, he found, the more a person claims to experience divine love the more likely that person is to spend time on charitable activities. But there was a significant exception, one that had to do with the presence (or absence) of a faith community: for those who did not attend services at church (or did so infrequently), the extent of their feeling loved by God had *no effect* on their service involvement. An experience of God's love issued forth in service to others only among regular church attenders. It is clear, then, that we need support from others in this calling to serve. And indeed, our twenty-four-hour survey suggests crucial ways in which other people play a role in our reaching out.

The Turn to Others

As we have noted, at least 16 percent (likely more) of our respondents claimed to have experienced within the past twenty-four hours loneliness powerful enough to register and remember. Part of this has to do, no doubt, with a culture that so atomizes persons that we see each other as individuals before we see each other as part of a family. "My father," recounts one friend of the authors, "belonged to an extended family of which all—bar one—lived within eighty miles of where he grew up." Americans have always been a mobile people, "almost nomadic," one historian termed us in 1888. Now, compounding our migratory tendencies, many of us are divorced, live hundreds of miles from offspring, and have strained relationships with parents. Two-career families mean both spouses are pushed to the edge of their margins routinely and are always pushed for time with friends. We have now so individualized our existence that we forfeit intimacies that give us richness that can be shared with others.

People spend more time in front of a TV screen or videocassette player than they do enjoying meals around a family table, or at church. Even the Internet, with its potential for linking cultures and people with similar interests, sometimes becomes a pale blue substitute for eye contact and real relationships.

And technology, with its enticements and draw on our attention, only compounds the isolation. People spend more time in front of a TV screen or videocassette player than they do enjoying meals around a family table, or at church. Even the Internet, with its potential for linking cultures and people with similar interests, sometimes becomes a pale blue substitute for eye contact and real relationships. One college president recounted that many of his students spend hours on the Internet: they will send e-mail to people down the dorm hall, communicating at a distance what once would have been said face-to-face, joining in chat rooms with people they could sit in the same room with. People end up starved for contact.

Such loneliness not only leaves Americans feeling bereft, it deprives them of experiences that strengthen them for service to others.We may have less contact with those who can enable us to live for higher ideals. When calling Americans to give more of themselves to others, it is crucial to realize the renewal they receive from ordinary relationships and spiritual fellowship. Certainly, as we have already noted, small groups play a significant role here. We also found that Americans turn to family and friends regularly for support. In our twenty-four-hour survey we asked, "Are the presence and support of others important to your religious faith or personal life?" Not surprisingly, 69 percent said yes. "Faith grows best in the presence of faith"

Seven in ten of our respondents said they need others in their faith journeys.

and service also grows best through others' modeling and inspiration. Seven in ten of our respondents said they need others in their faith journeys.

Who are these people whose presence and support matter so much? Our twenty-four-hour respondents overwhelmingly included family members (79 percent did so). Friends were next (52 percent). Then church members, pastors, and finally, each registering only a couple of responses, coworkers and neighbors. Family members, then, clearly provide much support to Americans' pursuit of spiritual growth. Says George Barna, "In many ways, the family will be the heart of the new Church. Today the typical family picks up the spiritual pieces after family members have had their exposure to a church, a parachurch ministry, TV, school, and various marketplace experiences."[5] Nothing can substitute for the family's role. No wonder that many ministers who specialize in ministry to youth realize they must also pay attention to the young person's family, not just the young person. Each person exists in a web of larger influences. Family wields tremendous power in shaping lives.

But church, whatever its potential for being sidelined in our culture's antiinstitutional mood, has a huge role, as well. Given Americans' high level of affiliation with religious congregations, it was no surprise that a majority (64 percent) of our respondents said yes when asked, "Do you happen to be a member of a church, synagogue, mosque, or other organized religious group?" Forty-four percent said they attended at least once a week. What other institution in America can claim such a following?

> When asked if they were members of a church, synagogue, mosque, or other organized group, 64 percent said yes.

People in churches sometimes question the effect of their nurture and witness. But it bears mentioning that people are influenced by others—like those found in churches—to an unseen and often unrealized degree. Acts of all kinds, like playing the violin, mastering the game of chess, or learning to paint, while solitary activities, nevertheless have a social dimension. We learn and practice these skills while building on the presence and example and inspiration of others. It is true, also, for acts of kindness and service. The pervasive influence of others—informal mentors, Sunday School teachers, pastors, church friends—live on in Americans' lives in sometimes forgotten ways. We still reap a kind of residual influence, even as churches worry about being marginalized in our semisecular times.

We will say more later about how churches can maximize their influence in society by capitalizing on the presence of so many people. For now we will note that a number of members are ready to be inspired and eager to be used for higher good. This will not happen automatically; the church must run counter to Madison Avenue's constant messages that the individual is the sum total of the universe. And people today are busier than ever; in his book *Faster* (subtitled "The Acceleration of Just About Everything"), James Gleick argues that despite all our time-saving strategies—instant credit, quick playback, microwave ovens—we are as impoverished in our relation to time as before. The church does not face a simple task when it contemplates calling people to greater involvement in helping others.

But some Americans, at least, are restless enough to ask deeper questions. Some need only the opportunity, the nudge of an invitation, a challenge from a pulpit, or the quiet modeling of a respected colleague. Corporations know this. Giants like Bell South and Maxwell House send employees on house-building projects sponsored by Habitat for Humanity or other charitable organizations. Public relations no doubt plays a role, but corporations also know that employees want to do more than pull down a paycheck. In this climate of attraction to "doing good," churches can help people catch a vision for a world beyond itself. And in a fragmented and impersonal society, churches can offer all kinds of opportunities for friendship and modeling that will strengthen countless members to do so.

Donald E. Miller tells the story of Monte Whittaker at the Vineyard Christian Fellowship in Anaheim, California. Whittaker helps lead his church's benevolence ministry. The work began simply when Whittaker and his wife noticed their poor neighbors in their rough L.A. neighborhood. They began handing out food in simple response to seeing hungry people. One night Whittaker felt led by God to some shacks along a nearby highway. The first family took a while to answer the door, he recalls: "There were about twelve people sleeping in this little room, so they had mattresses and blankets laid out through the whole thing, so when they opened the door, they had to lift a mattress to get the door open. And so we gave them most of what we had. . . ." The next door brought an encounter that affected Whittaker deeply: "I told [the next fellow] that we had free food that we were giving out, and he came back with a little baggie that had about a half inch of rice on the bottom of it. And he told me in Spanish that that was all the food he could spare because they only had another baggie about the same size left for his family, but that I was welcome to it." Whittaker explained that they wanted to give *him* food. "But this act of generosity," Miller notes, "so moved [Whittaker] that he and some friends from the Vineyard [Church] began taking groceries on a regular basis to the parks, and in a short time they were giving out several hundred bags weekly."

The ministry has grown, not surprisingly, to a warehouse where food is brought and sacks of it are given out, primarily to recent immigrants. Says Whittaker, "We need the poor a lot more than the poor need us. We need the poor in order to learn to become 'otherly.'" Whittaker believes that much of the health of his congregation springs from this faithful attention to the needy God placed in their path. [6]

The Impulse to Influence

We note finally the role of believers' influence through their efforts to talk about and model their faith and theological convictions. We observe these avenues of societal transformation less tangibly, perhaps, than acts of volunteering, but they too are full of transforming potential.

While most churches only perfunctorily encourage "faith sharing" or evangelism, already this quiet witness goes on in people's workplaces and homes and neighborhoods. Millions of Americans regularly share their religious convictions with their colleagues and neighbors and family members. While much more can be done, much already exists ready to be built on. In our survey, for example, we asked respondents if, in the last twenty-four hours, they had talked "to someone about God or some aspect of your faith or spirituality." Just over half (51 percent) said yes. A full quarter said they had counseled someone "from a spiritual perspective." People also felt free to allow their religious convictions to prompt discussion about a national issue. Nearly a quarter said they had. How interesting it would be to eavesdrop on some of these discussions—from abortion to tax hikes! Certainly many of the issues that face us as a nation have a profoundly moral component. Might not Christians who share biblically informed perspectives on the great social and political and economic issues make a difference? When asked if they had spoken out on a national issue out of religious convictions, 22 percent of our respondents said yes.

> When asked if they had spoken out on a national issue out of religious convictions, 22 percent of our respondents said yes.

The old taboo about discussing politics *and* religion seems to be fading. People seem more intrigued by spiritual matters and therefore more willing to broach angels and politics, healing and economics. Opportunities for sharing what Christians believe are not likely to shrivel up. Indeed, we see a number of churches adopting programs to reach out into their communities through phone campaigns, sophisticated direct-mail pieces, and simple neighbor-to-neighbor invitations.

To avoid being pushed to the margins of society amid the competing voices of commercialism and consumerism and me-ism, churches will have to continue to encourage such quiet efforts to be leaven and light. Paul wrote the early Roman believers, "How, then, can they call on the one they have not believed in? And how can they believe in the one of whom they have not heard? And how can they hear without someone preaching to them?" (Romans 10:14) How can postmoderns believe if someone does not speak? The church exists by its mission, someone once said, as a fire exists by burning. Thriving churches operate from a missionary mandate, not just a maintenance mode. They so enjoy God's goodness in Christ they feel compelled not to keep it to themselves.

Sharing the good news of Christianity comes not so much from buttonholing people in an office hallway or knocking on doors in what salesmen call cold-calling, but from what some call friendship evangelism, or lifestyle evangelism, or service evangelism. Which means opportunities usually come when we involve ourselves in others' lives and let our compassion open doors (sometimes literally) for a hearing. And with that hearing can come profound opportunities. What evangelicals call conversion or being born again or accepting Christ as Savior and Lord is not just one religious option. It is key to the transformation not only of individuals but of society. Believers will not only need to lend a hand but offer an invitation to truth, to the person of Jesus Himself.

Have Christians lost the missionary zeal that so propelled the earliest Christians and transformed the first-century world through their simple, heartfelt preaching? Americans tend to show a laissez-faire side toward other religious beliefs. Those in the so-called mainline denominations sometimes grow nervous around words such as *evangelism* or *outreach*. And some religious groups resent mightily the call to conversion from another faith. Certainly there is a place for gentle, loving sensitivity. But whatever the need for humility and respect for others, we cannot *not* reach out. A growing wave of what religion professor Donald E. Miller calls "new paradigm" churches (such as Monte Whittaker's Vineyard Christian Fellowship) refuses to separate compassion from witness, social action from evangelism. In this they continue in the stream of evangelicalism that has long given precedence to the message of salvation in Christ. They stress that more than new social programs are needed to turn around crime and poverty; no, they believe that a more fundamental change is needed—a changed heart and awakened soul as well as a hot lunch. The idea is not only to offer food to the famished, but to also share the Bread of Life, Jesus Himself, with the spiritually hungry.

Two models suggest the kind of possibilities that churches can seize in doing so.

The first is Habitat for Humanity. So far, Habitat has built 26,000 homes in the U.S. and over 45,000 homes internationally, often with the assistance of high-profile leaders such as Jimmy Carter. As a writer for *Christianity Today* reported, "Oprah [Winfrey] has sponsored homes. Congress has sponsored homes. Housewives have sponsored and built homes. Banks and Fortune 500 companies have sponsored homes." Asks the writer, "Why does Habitat build homes? 'Because of Jesus,'

says [founder Millard] Fuller. 'We are putting God's love into action.'"
For all the emphasis on the social benefits of adequate housing for the
poor, Fuller insists that this faith dimension not be stripped away:

> *I'm very sincere about this. . . . We need the*
> *evangelical influence in Habitat for Humanity.*
> *You can read all the literature about Habitat,*
> *and it is very plain that the Christian witness is*
> *very important. . . . [W]hat has happened is that*
> *Habitat has become popularized. . . . You've got*
> *people of every belief on earth watching [what*
> *we do]; but that's a wonderful opportunity. . . .*
> *When Oprah Winfrey gets on the tube and says,*
> *"Let's build some Habitat houses," thousands of*
> *people respond. Well, that's a glorious opportu-*
> *nity if we've got an organization in place thor-*
> *oughly infiltrated with dedicated Christians.*
> *Then these people will hear the Christian mes-*
> *sage. But if all the evangelicals have retreated to*
> *the sanctuary and have locked up the doors and*
> *they're back there meditating on Jesus behind*
> *stained-glass windows, where is the witness?* [7]

Then there is the Lighthouse movement. This somewhat loosely
affiliated network enlists families to reach out with the Christian message among their neighbors. Family members of a Lighthouse home
pray regularly for each person by name in the surrounding neighborhood houses, often creating opportunities for the praying families to
share their faith with neighbors. Churches and businesses and school
groups can also function as Lighthouses. Mission America, the group
spearheading the plan, says the strategy is to "pray, care, and share."
More than 350 national denominations and ministries collaborate.
Planners hope to see 100,000 local churches establish 3 million
Lighthouses which, they believe, could mean 260 million Americans

from coast to coast touched by prayer and evangelism. Participants begin praying for a few neighbors and show them acts of kindness, hospitality, and friendliness. As friendships develop, they look for opportunities to talk about their faith, distribute a video depicting the life of Christ or pamphlets with Christian themes, or invite them to attend church. [8] "This movement has no single source," says Paul Cedar of Mission America. "It's coming from local churches, denominations, and parachurch ministries. Over the last year and a half, more than 57 networks, 75 denominations, and 300 ministries have joined." The Lighthouse movement has become a major emphasis with the Southern Baptists, Assemblies of God, and other major denominations, he said. "One area of concern is the inner city, so we are directing more focus there."

The home of John Engen, station manager of KTIS radio in Minneapolis, is a Lighthouse. As one news story recounted:

> *As [Engen and his wife] stroll through the neighborhood, people ask them what they are doing, and they explain that they are praying. "Now instead of being strangers, we are getting to know each other again." Engen put a Lighthouse sticker in a window and "the next day a person drove up and hugged me and said, 'Thank you for being a Lighthouse.'". . . Christians have "cocooned ourselves into a coma," Engen said. "What [the Lighthouse movement] is doing is simple stuff. If we want spiritual substance we must pray and love [people] into the Kingdom [of God.]"[9]*

Will the efforts help Americans overcome the problems that beset the nation? Not if confined only to middle-class suburban neighborhoods. Not if good deeds are not joined with deeper solutions and not if spiritual lessons are not made credible with concrete acts of caring.

However Americans reach out, through bags of groceries or evangelistic conversations, through homeless shelters like Charles Strobel's or through citywide crusades, three groups are likely to have a crucial role in the coming century, three groups to which we now turn our attention.

THREE GROUPS TO WATCH

"[Most of] what I had known about [Philadelphia's] African-American population was cast in terms of problems—problems of drugs, . . . crime, . . . poverty. We went to the black churches in the city [and] I saw some of the most healthy, vibrant communities I'd ever seen in my life."

—JOHN DiIULIO [1]

MARGIE DENNIE WILL tell you: twenty-five years ago you would have been pressed to find an African-American in the Baptist General Conference. Then congregations in the denomination around the country found their neighborhoods changing. African-Americans began moving into what had been Anglo strongholds. The Baptist General Conference, with historical roots ultimately stretching back centuries to Sweden, realized they faced a choice. Would they follow the "white flight" and relocate in new suburbs? Or embrace the shifting racial demographics and welcome blacks into their corporate life?

Margie Dennie provides a partial answer. With bright eyes and a smile that flashes white teeth against dark skin, she will tell you that she found her way into the historically white Baptist denomination thirteen years ago. An African-American with family roots in the Deep South, she even married a Baptist preacher, also black, who was called by denominational officials to start a new black and multicultural church in the suburbs of Tampa. Now you can find her at her husband's church, or mothering their three school-age children, or teaching sixth grade at the local public school. Years ago, when we profiled her in our book *The Saints Among Us,* she had returned to a Chicago area college to get her teaching certificate. Now with that behind her and a teaching job landed, her work, she believes, has become a kind of mission itself. "I'm coming to realize the importance of 'being there' for my students. Even praying for them. They go through so many things these days. I want to tell them there's hope when they get down or discouraged or need to question."

She also sees the world through God-filtered lenses. She believes such faith comes naturally from her African-American heritage. "We grow up in a subculture with strong concern for the spiritual life and very strong reverence for God," she says. "Faith is a strong value. The hardship of slavery must be a part of that. The way families pass along concern for the soul is also part of it. But it really is part of our whole black experience—the way God chose to allow the prejudice to exist, and then deliver boldly as He did through those active in the Civil Rights movement." She has modest aspirations for her own life. But she believes she is part of something much larger. "God uses my life in small ways I know I won't see results from till years from now. Some I may never see. But every now and then I get a glimpse."

Melting-Pot Spirituality

America has long displayed something of the racial color and culture of the world. So has American spirituality. From African-American spirituals to Latin masses, from Latin American Christmas customs to

Jewish holiday foods, the nation's religious life has been fed by wide diversity. "Red and yellow, black and white," children learn to sing in Sunday School, "they are precious in His sight."

> America has long displayed something of the racial color and culture of the world. So has American spirituality.

Our nation's wide range of ages and racial backgrounds suggests more than variety. It also points to influences that lie ahead. A number of population groups will shape America's next spirituality in dramatic ways. To the surprise of many, three groups—including African-Americans like Margie Dennie—may have more to do with the health of our communities and churches than any others. As their influence grows, they will change the nation and alter the ways we pray and minister.

First, though, a word about groups we will not single out. Certainly women, long the backbone of churches and a volunteer core in every community, can be expected increasingly to have a leadership voice in both the political and religious sphere. More women than men go to church, pray, and say religion is important in their lives. In surveys women register higher in levels of personal belief, just as has likely been true from the earliest centuries of Christianity, when women figured significantly, serving as witnesses to Jesus' resurrection, teaching, hosting house churches, nurturing family members in the faith. But we will reserve a detailed exploration of their special contribution to contemporary American spirituality to others.

And one could cite a number of ethnic groups that will continue to affect life in the new millennium. Demographers expect Hispanics and Asians to fuel most U.S. population growth over the next fifty years. Always a nation of immigrants, America is now home to one-fifth of the world's Hispanic peoples. American cities host some of the largest Spanish-speaking populations in the world. The cultural impact has already been substantial. Reports *Newsweek* magazine, "Like the arrival of European immigrants at the turn of the [twentieth] century, the tide of Hispanic immigrants—and the fast growth of Latino families—has injected a new energy into the nation's cities. Latinos are changing the way the country looks, feels and thinks, eats, dances and votes." [2] And because Hispanics represent the youngest population group in the U.S., as the younger generations mature, the process of multiplication will continue to change the face of our nation. "In less than one life span," notes the Web site of the parachurch organization Navigators, "Americans from racial and ethnic minority groups will outnumber those of Anglo-Saxon descent." [3] What changes will such shifts prompt? Whatever the race or ethnic group, whether we think of Jewish or Native American, Asian or Indian, no longer can we expect to live in a monochrome culture. From a God's-eye view, white Anglo-Saxon Protestants have never cornered the kingdom of God. And spirituality, already drawing from centuries of scattered cultures and amalgamated languages and music and art, will continue to enjoy the rich and varied benefits.

In particular, however, we want to look at one group that registers remarkable readings on opinion surveys, and then examine two age groups that also have potential to blaze a new trail in the third millennium.

Group 1: The Soul of Black Americans

It could be said that African-Americans such as Margie Dennie set the pace for people of all colors in this country. They are arguably the most religious people in the world. History plays a part in this. In the days before their nineteenth-century emancipation from slavery, the Christian faith told slaves that they were not just white man's property, but more than anything children of God. Belief provided not only words of comfort, but a compelling source of personal empowerment. Now, it seems impossible to find a black woman or man who does not believe in God. Consider:

- Virtually 100 percent of blacks believe in God or a higher power, compared to 95 percent of whites.

- Six in ten blacks (62 percent) "completely agree" with the statement, "I am sometimes very conscious of the presence of God." This compares with far fewer whites (44 percent).

- Ninety-one percent of African-Americans say that God has guided them in making a decision; the figure for whites is 81 percent.

- Ninety-four out of every one hundred blacks believe that Jesus is the Son of God, compared to 82 percent for whites.

- Blacks are more likely than whites to say they are dissatisfied with the nation's moral climate.

- Religion has more saliency for blacks than for whites, with 83 percent saying they believe religion "can answer the problems of today" compared with 58 percent among whites.

In *The Saints Among Us* we shared how we found that blacks were twice as likely to fit our profile of the highly spiritually committed. Indeed, many "saints" come from what society considers the least recognized and marginally powerful group: the nonwhite, female, uneducated poor.

> Many "saints" come from what society considers the least recognized and marginally powerful group: the nonwhite, female, uneducated poor.

Blacks' strong spiritual profile does not come only from individual beliefs and practices. Note:

- Fifty-four percent of blacks attended church in a test week, compared to 42 percent of whites.

- Seventy-eight percent of blacks claim church membership, compared to 68 percent of whites.

- Estimates of black churches range as high as 70,000, suggesting in sheer numbers a social phenomenon of often unremarked-on strength.

Given the emphasis on evangelism and outreach of many black

> Given the emphasis on evangelism and outreach of many black churches, we believe black churches could become the crucible for renewal of American faith and the wider society.

churches, we believe black churches could become the crucible for renewal of American faith and the wider society. They provide community, grounding in biblical truth, and sometimes fiery spiritual intensity. No wonder David Bryant, president of America's National Prayer Committee, says that some of the great dynamic impetus for prayer movements in this country will come from the urban black churches.

But we see a huge problem: Christianity's history is not typically color-blind. Blatant prejudice has at times stranded white middle-class churches from the contagion of faith experienced by other groups. Churches tend to be among the most segregated institutions in the country. We have few equivalents to the "integrated busing" programs public schools use (note some suggestions along these lines in chapter 7).

But why should the spiritual vibrancy of black churches not spread new vitality to white churches? And vice versa? Can the suburban churchly enclave recognize that the urban black church, while not perfect, has much to teach? One challenge to the church of the twenty-first century, then, will be to break down walls that separate. "If you can't have humility to be in balance with others," says jazz trumpeter Wynton Marsalis, "you won't be as good a jazz musician as you might be." [4] Much the same can be said about tending to spiritual growth. We do not need to board jets to far-flung regions to broaden our vision for faith and ministry and service. Within our borders, in the neighborhood next door, ministry can be a cross-subcultural experience to the enrichment of all.

Group 2: The Millennial Generation

"Slackers." That is the term the high school principal spits out at Marty McFly and his young friends in the *Back to the Future* movie series. Surveys reveal that many American adults hold such negative views. Teens today frequently feel their elders malign, misunderstand, or simply ignore them. They hear adjectives such as "immoral," "reckless," and "untrustworthy." In contrast to those tempted to this stereotype of youth, we believe that America's young people represent energy, talent, passion for authenticity, and spiritual hunger. Two decades of the Gallup Youth Survey, with more than 1,100 weekly reports sent to the Associated Press, provide a cumulative snapshot of the greatly needed qualities our nation's young people can bring us, as well as areas for concern.

For one thing, this is a group to watch for their sheer numbers. Approximately 40 percent of the world's population is nineteen or younger. The number of children and youth alive today exceeds the entire world's population in 1950. And in America a segment of teens, the generation born between 1982 and 2003 (sometimes called the millennial generation because the first wave will graduate from high school in the year 2000), includes more children and youth in school than any other cohort in U.S. history. Attendance figures for schools will continue to rocket through 2008. The multiplied millions of young people will drastically influence the shape of world culture as it emerges over the next ten years.

But it is more than numbers. There are generational characteristics that demand our attention. This is not a generation consumed by greed, for example, contrary to images of youth wanting only to burn through bucks at the mall or make a killing in business after graduation. Survey after survey shows that teens have a keen interest in helping people who are less fortunate than they are, especially in their own communities. They may need grounding in personal morality more than some earlier generations, but if our nation is less polluted, racist, sexist, and more peace loving, we can thank young people who lead the edge of these trends.

> Survey after survey shows that teens have a keen interest in helping people who are less fortunate than they are, especially in their own communities.

Far from being clueless about the world around them, the great majority of teenagers often discuss philosophical and spiritual questions with their friends. Ethical questions about what is right to do and what is wrong top the list of serious questions that teens discuss among themselves. Nearly half (45 percent) say they often try to sort out right and wrong in conversation with their friends while an additional 37 percent say they sometimes hold discussions on ethical matters. Six percent say the topic never comes up.

When it comes to asking the even larger questions about who we are, what life means, and how we should understand the universe, 20 percent (one in five) discuss these matters with friends "often," with another 37 percent saying they "sometimes" do. On the other hand, 44 percent say they rarely or never discuss these matters. Those most likely to discuss these matters are young women, teens age sixteen and older, and students doing above average work in school. Spiritual questions about whether God exists and if there is life after death command the attention of a majority of teenagers.

Spiritual questions about whether God exists and if there is life after death command the attention of a majority of teenagers.

Further, young people say they are enthusiastic about helping others, willing to work for peace and a healthy world, and feel positive about their teachers. Says Episcopal youth minister Cynthia Seeliger, "Kids today are really servant oriented. I sometimes get calls from kids saying 'Can I volunteer? Can you recommend a project?' They need to do a service project for their school honor society. But they volunteer not just to fulfill a requirement but because they want to. I know a number who are choosing their college based on what service opportunities it offers." Indeed, nearly half of all young people today volunteer. Half of all schools have a volunteer program. A majority of young people would like to see such programs become mandatory. And no generation in history has seen more students go on short-term mission trips around the world. In the 1980s, says Roger Peterson, director of Short Term Evangelical Missions, thousands went. In the 1990s the figure hit the hundreds of thousands. [5]

Teens also want clear rules to live by; they want clarity. They favor teaching values in schools, which half of schools now do. Teens in sex education classes overwhelmingly would like abstinence to be taught. Young women would like more help in saying "no" to sexual advances. Large majorities say they are happy and excited about the future, say they are likely to marry, say they want to have children, and desire to reach the top of their chosen careers.

Yet youth are also threatened on all sides.

Many young people in the homes of both the privileged and under-privileged worry daily about their physical well-being. One teenager in four is worried about his or her safety level at school each day.

Young people are apprehensive about the future and a host of problems that are relatively new on the scene: the threat of AIDS, the availability of potentially deadly drugs, and random death and violence, to name a few. Gone for many youth are the key support systems that have been important to child-rearing and a young person's sense of security: strong families, friendly and support-ive neighborhoods, and a society generally in agreement on vital, core issues.

> Gone for many youth are the key support systems that have been important to child-rearing and a young person's sense of security: strong families, friendly and supportive neighborhoods, and a society generally in agreement on vital, core issues.

Youth also face risks from themselves. Less than half of America's teens (43 percent) believe it is important to have a deep religious faith. Just as many teens (44 percent) believe that having lots of money is important to them. They rate friends, home, school, music, and television ahead of religion and books as having the greatest influence on their generation.

What can be predicted as a result of such external pressures and internal weak points? A report from the Carnegie Council on Adolescent Development states, "All together, nearly half of American adolescents are at high or moderate risk of seriously damaging their life chances. The damage may be near-term, or it may be delayed, like a time-bomb." The report notes that these conditions exist among families of all income levels and backgrounds—in cities, suburbs, and rural areas. But they are especially severe in neighborhoods of concentrated poverty, where adolescents are more likely to lack two prerequisites for healthy growth and development: a close relationship with a dependable adult and the perception of meaningful opportunities in mainstream America. And while a "dependable adult" is a good step, nothing replaces a mother and father for providing a caring, secure environment.

These factors suggest both the challenge and the opportunity for Americans wanting to make the most of this rising generation. To do so will require understanding that today's youth come with their own needs and unique strengths. It will require noticing fundamental changes in our culture and youth subculture. The changes are so great, in fact, that Dean Borgman, professor of youth ministry at Gordon-Conwell Theological Seminary, says Y2K kids represent the "second great watershed" for youth culture. [6] And the repercussions carry great implications for how religious communities reach out to (and reach) young people.

> Dean Borgman, professor of youth ministry at Gordon-Conwell Theological Seminary, says Y2K kids represent the "second great watershed" for youth culture.

The first watershed, says Borgman, happened in the forties, when the idea of youth culture arose in the first place. Following the Depression and World War II, young people found themselves with free time, money to spend, and energy. Football teams, cheerleaders, bobby socks, and loud music coalesced with a new sense of youthful identity. Ministry to such young people, often needing entertainment on Saturday nights, gave birth to the youth rally, which combined lively musical performances with evangelistic messages. Youth for Christ, Young Life, and others made persistent use of the rally. [7]

But that was all before the advent of television and video. In the early eighties, the entertainment media began to effect a cultural shift. No longer could you say music expressed or conveyed the culture of youth. It *was* the culture. The decline of the family coincided with this electronic revolution. Says Borgman, "Their Walkmans, VCRs, cable TV [to say nothing of computers to come] have given these kids an artificial and superficial home in the absence of parents." They are plugged in like no generation before them. And therefore susceptible to a culture that is so all-pervasive they cannot escape it. Here is how writer Wendy Murray Zoba summarized some experts' take on youth:

■ This generation's pulse runs fast. Bombarded by frequent images, they are in need of continual "hits."
■ The [TV/VCR] remote control symbolizes their reality: change is constant; focus is fragmented.
■ They've eaten from the tree of knowledge.
■ They live for now.
■ They are jaded. Nothing shocks them.
■ They are a cyber-suckled community.
■ They process concepts in narrative images (like Nike commercials).
■ Their [bull] detectors are always on.
■ They don't trust adults.

Helping kids discern the false messages amid the amniotic fluid of constant visual and auditory bombardment will pose a major challenge. Says Zoba: "This generation is growing up with access to information far beyond that of any previous generation (except for those who cannot afford technology). Computers and the media have brought the world home. Unfortunately, there may not be caring adults to help youth sort through this information to discern what is valuable and accurate." [8]

But as we will see, the information age provides believers with a powerful vehicle for communicating truth. Given the majority of young people's interest in the larger questions and their hunger for truth, there is much to build on. Engagement with them means more than using tired tools while ignoring the wired technology that pervades their existence. In reaching out, we must not regard them as pathologies waiting to happen, but sparks of joy to be fanned aflame and nurtured. After all, a remarkable two out of three teens (67 percent) say they feel in their lives a need to experience spiritual growth. More than eight in ten say that they consider their religious beliefs very important to them. Their religious impulse will not go away. It awaits simply to be nourished and given the appropriate attention.

We will say more later about opportunities for grounding in biblical literacy and ethical savvy, but for now we note the suggestions of some, such as futures thinker and church consultant Richard Kew of the Anglican Forum for the Future, that youth are just waiting to be challenged, just waiting for opportunities to do more with their lives than play Nintendo or watch MTV. Kew, for example, argues for denominations and other faith-based groups to create Youth Volunteer Corps:

> *As I was pondering and praying over such a scheme as this the other afternoon I went out to walk on the running track near my home. As I came out of the door I saw a pair of young Mormon missionaries walk by. I greeted them and then watched as a van came along to pick them up and take them back to where they were living. I am profoundly impressed by the manner in which the Mormons equip their young to share the message of Joseph Smith; they put us to shame. We need to develop a similar kind of program in the [church], a program that will challenge our young people to set aside a year or two of their lives for sacrificial service, either here or overseas.*

Group 3: The Preretirement Army

As it happens, much the same could be said about the third and final group we profile that is poised to make a profound difference: the preretirement group (and, by extension, those already retired). Many churches have given little thought to this changing demographic, and have yet to wake up to the enormous impact this group (sometimes called Builders or the Builder generation) can shortly have, if nurtured and called forth to share their time, talents, and considerable material abundance. While the preretirement group is poised to make a profound difference in our society, many congregations have given little thought to this changing demographic.

> While the preretirement group is poised to make a profound difference in our society, many congregations have given little thought to this changing demographic.

Advances in medical science contribute to this millennial moment of opportunity. No longer does retirement automatically come with a drop-off in physical stamina. Persons in the fifty to sixty-four age range are a high-energy group. Many have skills and wisdom that are unsurpassed. They are all dressed up, in a way, with nowhere to go. Indeed, recounts Jimmy and Rosalyn Carter in the book *Everything to Gain,* which highlights their departure from White House life, retirement can present people with new dreams, new challenges to conquer. [9] This group of almost-retired (and already-retired) are poised to make a major contribution to the betterment of U.S. society. Their potential looms large if its members can abandon the mindset that they should be winding down and instead grasp the concept that their lives and careers to date are only a prelude to what is to come. They can picture more than visiting grandchildren or ticking off miles in an RV or spending time at the golf course. At retirement they can move from success to significance, to use author and businessman Robert Buford's phrase. (See Buford's book *Halftime.*)

As with youth, their sheer numbers are significant: persons in the fifty to sixty-four age group account for about one fifth of our population, at least ten million. Almost half (48 percent) of this group describe their health as "excellent" or "very good," only slightly less than the figure for the nation as a whole. One fourth have graduated from college and half of those have done graduate work.

And their understanding of spirituality suggests a wealth of faith and wisdom. Seven in ten say that religion is either the most important or a very important influence in their lives, a higher percentage than that recorded for younger Americans. Compared to all other age groups, persons in this age group are most likely to say that their lives "belong to God or a higher power." A call to higher goals in life will play on hearts already made receptive by a faith that counsels concern for neighbor and selfless giving.

Roughly half already engage in some form of volunteer work, in these ways:

■ Helping older people	72%
■ Church or religious programs	63%
■ Children or youth groups	42%
■ Sports or recreational programs	31%
■ School or public education programs	28%
■ Housing, shelter, and aid to the homeless	28%
■ Environmental projects	24%

No wonder people in this age group frequently name Billy Graham and Jimmy Carter as role models; they find religion important and they admire those who go beyond doing well (as in well-off) to doing *good*.

This perception is key for how preretirement Americans view what is to come. They picture the world better off in several areas in the year 2025: quality of life, lifestyles of the rich, race relations, medical care availability, and a smaller percentage of families where both parents are unemployed. They see the world getting worse, however, in these respects: life for the poor and middle class, moral values in society, threats of terrorism, the crime rate, and the quality of the environment. Indeed, on the whole this group is rather glum in their predictions, underscoring the need for these people to be involved in a major way in trying to reverse the negative developments they foresee. And there will be challenges in enlisting more of them; this aging population faces family structures so frayed that many can expect to spend their senior years alone. Some may fight a temptation to retreat. But the potential is great.

Frank Nicodem provides an illustration of the possibilities. He calls himself "semiretired" but he can hardly be called inactive. He was raised in India the son of missionaries, and after a stint in World War II he began selling insurance in 1950, eventually cofounding Central Security Mutual Insurance Company. He also points to many rich experiences through the years "serving Christ" through various Christian organizations. But "retirement" did not mean an end to his service to God and others. He went to a missions organization (The Evangelical Alliance Mission—TEAM) to see if he could offer his experience. TEAM sent him to Madrid to help found a new seminary. That done and once back in the States, Nicodem and his wife, along with five other couples, helped start a new congregation in the western suburbs of Chicago.

Nicodem began to believe God was "laying on his heart" a message for others in his age stage that "God was not through with them yet." He called an old friend who was facing retirement and out of their conversations a new organization was born: Christian Association of Prime Timers. CAP is a "Christian alternative" to the American Association of Retired People (AARP), but with a twist. Along with the normal discount programs on prescription drugs and a bed-and-breakfast travel club, CAP provides "challenging opportunities where members can use their gifts and talents to advance the kingdom of God." Its Servant Opportunities Network, for example, tracks more than six thousand short-term and long-term volunteer openings, both domestic and overseas.

Nicodem tells stories of how some denominations have caught the vision: the Lutheran Church, Missouri Synod, for example, has a group called Laborers for Christ. The program for seniors has built more than 600 church buildings or facility additions. The seniors come to sites in RVs and work moderate hours four days a week, have time for sightseeing, and then come back in the evenings to campfire services and old-time hymn sings. "They go home," says Nicodem, "feeling as though they have done something constructive for the kingdom of Christ. You don't have to be an electrician to pull wires through walls under an electrician's supervision. Lots of people can hold wallboard in place while someone nails it."

When Hurricane Waldo hit, a large evangelical denomination turned out eight thousand seniors to help. Says Nicodem: "When helping clean up after the devastation, sometimes people would ask the volunteers, 'Why are you doing this?' And they would answer, 'God loved you enough to tell us to come here to help.' Through servanthood they opened the door to witness. That captures what I love to see happen. I'm trying to get people to pitch in and use their time constructively for God's kingdom in what is the prime time of their lives."

In light of such possibilities, Richard Kew puts the challenge like this: "We need to multiply opportunities for this group to use their senior years in gospel service, bringing their skills and gifts to the task of the fulfillment of the Great Commission. . . . If we do not offer them opportunities, they will not take them."

This gift of time and talent also links to a treasure of monetary resources. Some seniors, of course, pinch pennies and worry about money enough for simple meals. But overall, estimates of the accumulated wealth of seniors all range high: in the trillions. Such is about to be passed along to another generation. But surely some of it can and should be, through planned giving, set loose in a country and wider world in vast need of resources. Sometimes some simple information, a gentle invitation, or financial advice are all that is needed to ensure that seniors give gifts that keep on giving, long after they are gone.

> Estimates of the accumulated wealth of seniors all range high: in the trillions. Such is about to be passed along to another generation. But surely some of it can and should be, through planned giving, set loose in a country and wider world in vast need of resources.

The Future in Action

One stunning example of the potential to be realized from all three groups comes from Boston. The Rev. Eugene Rivers has much to do with it. *Newsweek* magazine called the African-American "an impolitic preacher on the cutting edge of a hot idea: can religion fight crime and save kids?"[10] Rivers points to profound results from a partnership of churches and youth and volunteers in Dorchester, a tough, crime-ridden section of Boston. With church leaders from thirty-nine churches in the Boston area joining forces with law enforcement agencies and other groups, at-risk youth were identified and offered an alternative to their destructive and deadly choices. These youth were brought into a relationship with those dedicated to their restoration. Groups offering job training and remedial measures to get these youth back to school are part of the ongoing process. Rivers believes religious faith can fight crime and save young people. Statistics bear him out. For one two-year period Boston had only one gun-related homicide committed by a juvenile.

The story is one that should be heeded by Americans who sequester themselves behind gated communities or plan retirement as an escape. It suggests the power of a partnership that can include the preretirement and retirement crowd with wonderful opportunities for all three of the groups we have profiled in this chapter. A partnership that will change the face of the nation if we heed the call and do not neglect the possibilities.

WHAT SHOULD WE DO?: WORKING SPIRITUALITY DOWN DEEP

"Contemporary spirituality desperately needs focus, precision, and roots: focus on Christ, precision in the Scriptures, and roots in a healthy tradition. . . . As we get it straight ourselves, we will be equipped to provide leadership to others, an evangelical *leadership that is so conspicuously lacking at present."*
—EUGENE PETERSON [1]

A N ATMOSPHERE OF striking earnestness pervades Pantego Bible Church. The evangelical congregation, recently occupied with a building program to accommodate its expanding membership, sits amid the unremarkable terrain of the Dallas-Fort Worth Metroplex. But even apart from its energetic commitment to move into new quarters, a visitor can tell it is a church on a mission.

Leaders of the congregation have a new "passion" to transform people into "fully developing followers of Christ."

The latter phrase has so captured the corporate focus that in everyday conversation leaders use a shorthand version: FDFC. Under the leadership of Randy Frazee, senior pastor, and the prompting of Bob Buford of Leadership Network, for two years the church's elders, staff, and "outside consultants" debated and prayed about potential "trademarks" of a follower of Christ, the FDFC. Through meetings with members and high-profile Christian leaders such as Buford and Dallas Willard, staff members confirmed their convictions that it was not enough to succeed at the so-called ABCs of church ministry: attendance, building, cash. They knew that spiritual formation had to do with more than promoting churchgoing and encouraging "quiet times" at set periods of the day. They decided they wanted to become a place and a people focused on the Great Commandment of Jesus in Luke 10:27: to love God with all one's heart and to love one's neighbor as one's own self. But what would that look like? What would such an intentional goal mean for their programming and corporate life? They wanted members who knew what they believed, knew how to pray, and knew how to live with compassion in a damaged world.

They understood this would require something other than church life as usual. So they developed a list of what they somewhat inelegantly called "core competencies," key areas of discipleship for a believer. And they divided them along classical lines: beliefs (theological essentials), practices (spiritual disciplines), and virtues (habits of being and relating). They developed a survey for each person to help people gauge progress, called a Christian Life Profile. Members filled it out for themselves and, even more daunting, asked friends and family and colleagues to rate them on various aspects of faith and virtue. The hope is, they say, "that these thirty core ideas will not only assist individuals in targeting their spiritual growth but will also create a common language for followers of Christ to gather in community and talk about their spiritual lives." Possibly, Randy Frazee and others at Pantego Bible Church believe, "this kind of dialogue can incite a contagious faith that will touch the world with the life of Christ within us."

However far they go in meeting their goals, whether their experiment catches on (they are developing materials for what they hope will be hundreds of thousands of other churches and believers who want to join the "movement"), their urgency will do well to carry them into the early decades of the new millennium. They are determined to do more than slip quietly into the margins of an irrelevant faith.

We believe that as spirituality continues to capture the attention of Americans, the task of defining truth will grow more pressing. We will need to learn to do more than simply baptize the consumerist and me-centered and morally flabby values of secular culture. Religious groups do not always realize this. It is a time, says Eugene Peterson, of drift and dilettantism. Our culture's tendencies, while welcoming to spirituality, often have a diffusing, fuzzying effect. It grows harder to insist on solid truths and tradition and rock-hard integrity. "Historically," Peterson says, "evangelical Christians have served the church by bringing sharpness and ardor to matters of belief and behavior, insisting on personal involvement, injecting energy and passion, returning daily to the Scriptures for command and guidance, and providing communities of commitment. But presently there is not an equivalent precision in matters of spirituality. It turns out that we have been affected by our secularizing culture far more than we had realized." [2]

Evangelical churches, of course, are not the only ones affected, nor the only ones with a heritage that can help us greet the challenges of the twenty-first century with clarity. For all who agonize about nurturing faith in changing times, we turn our attention to what can be done. In this chapter we look at strategies within the boundaries of congregational life, ways to pass on faith to the members and children of our communities. It is a task, as we will see, not to be left to mere chance. A task for which we can already discern clear areas for focus.

Formation Focus 1:
Grounding Faith in Revealed Truth

As we have suggested, America's next spirituality will exhibit great openness to, even greater eagerness for, spiritual growth. Nothing suggests this will change in the near future. Our twenty-four-hour survey confirmed this. We asked, "Would you say you are seeking to grow in your religious faith, or not?" The proportion saying yes, only slightly less than those who said they felt a need in their lives for spiritual growth, was three-quarters (76 percent). We also asked if people had a sense during their day of "God being loving." More than two-thirds said yes. Only 9 percent said they had a sense of God being angry. People generally connect faith with positive emotions.

> When asked if respondents had a sense during the day of "God being loving," 70 percent said yes. Only 9 percent said they had a sense of God being angry.

For all we hear of people who feel rejected by God or kept at a distance by divine wrath, most people in our survey seemed positively disposed.

This core of congeniality provides a starting point. Americans, for all the media's caricatures of believers as legalists and soured grouches, have a mostly friendly attitude toward religion. But that general warmth is indeed just a starting point. Faith in America is broad but not deep. The average American's vague sense of "the good Lord" often lacks definition. Sometimes adults' faith bears the barnacles of childhood misconceptions. Nursery pictures of Jesus meek and mild do not exhaust the full range of theologically sound belief. God is more than a vague transcendence or a kindly feeling that greets fellow believers when they meet. Historic faith says that cherubic angels who guard a child's crib or stealth angels who rescue stranded motorists provide only part of the picture. The God of Judeo-Christian tradition has vigorous qualities that have been made known and need articulation.

> Faith in America is broad but not deep. The average American's vague sense of "the good Lord" often lacks definition.

Americans long for a meaningful spirituality, and the task of the church is to ground that desire in the concrete truth of God's Word.

Adults who shed many of their faulty perceptions about other areas of life remain curiously uninformed in matters of faith and views of God; their stages of spiritual maturation do not follow their stages of emotional maturation. And this points to a serious weakness in much current spirituality: our culture denies the value of careful reflection on matters of belief.

It is not just the sheer noise and speed and volume of images and sounds that rush at us from video screens or boom boxes. We see a determined effort not to say too much about God's actual nature or expectations for belief or discipleship. It falls on postmodern ears as a theological imperialism curiously out of fashion. This requires sustained and immediate remedying. Mike Regele and Mark Schulz write, "As the institutional church faces the unfolding of the twenty-first century, it faces a great challenge. In the postmodern world, there is a 'reality for every occasion.' The church's message is simply one more voice in the cacophony of created realities to attract a following." [3] Many in our culture prefer to leave God matters undefined or left to an individual's own devising. Personal interpretation reigns supreme. Leaders in some circles worry more about letting people "tell their own story" than ensuring that they have heard and comprehended the Bible's Great Story.

> Leaders in some circles worry more about letting people "tell their own story" than ensuring that they have heard and comprehended the Bible's Great Story.

The problem is not so much that people do not believe anything; it is that they believe everything, says Lynn Garrett, religion editor of *Publishers Weekly,* a magazine for book publishers and bookstore owners. This is unlikely to change soon. "Where is spirituality going?" asks Garrett. "It's going everywhere. There are many niches and subcultures in our society, including religious ones. I don't see any of them going away—if anything, they will multiply. And in our 'thirty-one-flavors' culture, the many books we at *Publishers Weekly* refer to in-house as 'generic spirituality' have been bleached of all sectarian elements, to make them palatable for the greatest number of people."

The emphasis is on a desired feeling or fleeting moment of wonder, not on understanding truths with a larger view or power to truly transform. Sensation and subjective experience is so prized that what a person actually believes recedes in importance. Joel Belz of *World* magazine speaks of "an apparent determination by most people in our society to believe as many different things as they possibly can, all at the same time, and even if some of those things flatly contradict one another."[4]

It helps to know this, but that does not mean we will always find our efforts met with easy acquiescence. One youth pastor tells of a visiting student who had come with a regular youth group member. She seemed to enjoy the group's activities. "But after I wrote an article in our teen newsletter about truth, she stopped coming. I approached her about why, and it became evident that she was greatly offended that I would suggest that all people should follow biblical principles. She said each person should have the freedom to do what he or she wanted, and no one should be able to tell another what to believe."[5]

Respect for others' views will always have a place in the church, of course. But in our current climate, tolerance becomes an unwillingness to declare anything true or compelling. It will become increasingly difficult to argue for *a* truth that somehow has meaning above competing claims for truth. But no less essential. What people believe *matters.* In *The Ground and Grammar of Theology,* professor Thomas Torrance demonstrates that the church's preaching and teaching in the first five centuries of the Christian era effected a monumental change in the world's thinking—massive shifts in both scientific perception and moral viewpoint. The content of that faith was not neutral in that powerful effort. Not all beliefs about God are equally healthy or salutary.

The calling to preach and teach, then, will only become more crucial in the new millennium. A key goal must be to develop biblical literacy among religious communities' own members. Surveys remind us of the pressing need. Americans revere the Bible but do not typically read it. A 1999 Gallup survey found that 38 percent of American adults read the Bible weekly or more often (close to the figure for 1990, which was 40 percent). The percentage of persons with a college education has more than tripled since the Gallup poll was founded in 1935, but the level of biblical knowledge appears to have hardly budged.

By biblical literacy we mean more than knowing what biblical character said what phrase in what historical period, but understanding in a profound way basic tenets about God, a kind of theological ABCs that allows people to comprehend the profound truths of Christian faith. For those of us who are Christians, how many people in our churches understand what it means to say Jesus died on the cross for our redemption and salvation? How many understand that the resurrection of Jesus is more than a symbol we celebrate at Easter along with Easter bunnies? Similar questions could be leveled at the rank and file of other faith communities. Many Americans do not know what they believe, or why. Many do not know what it means to belong to the faith or denomination to which they subscribe. They would be hard-pressed to defend their faith, if called on.

Many "born-again" Christians, to cite another example, while more orthodox in their beliefs and more faithful in churchgoing, differ little from other Americans on a number of non-Christian beliefs, such as reincarnation, witches, ghosts, and channeling. Born-again citizens (who account for four in ten in Gallup surveys) are as likely as their counterparts to believe in astrology, consult astrology charts, and to have consulted a fortune-teller. A national survey of Protestantism conducted by Search, a Minneapolis survey research company, revealed that only 32 percent of mainline denominational church members have an "integrated" or mature faith, "marked by both a deep, personal relation to a loving God and a consistent devotion to serving others." The low level of biblical

> A national survey of Protestantism conducted by Search, a Minneapolis survey research company, revealed that only 32 percent of mainline denominational church members have an "integrated" or mature faith, "marked by both a deep, personal relation to a loving God and a consistent devotion to serving others."

knowledge is only partly the fault of the education programs of churches and religious communities in the country. While parents certainly play a key role, only one-third of teenagers are currently receiving religious training of any sort, whether in church, school, or home. Is it any wonder that religious knowledge seems so anemic?

Granted, the church has fallen at times into a dry, overly cognitive orthodoxy that does not feed the heart or imagination. And our times favor the keenness of experiences over beliefs, emotions more than propositions. But there are some truths so basic to a healthy faith that we cannot blithely leave them to personal interpretation or private embellishment. Sometimes we need more than someone telling us to find out what we "feel" or what sounds good (as though our sporadic training in home and church and school or from the latest talk show therapist-guru has equipped us with adequate theological categories for spiritual discernment). No, we will continue to need to articulate clearly and earnestly the reason for the hope within us (1 Peter 3:15), not just to unbelievers, but to those who number themselves among our religious communities.

This is more than an exercise in making a solo spiritual "journey," that word so in vogue in spirituality circles. Sometimes in our teaching and preaching and informal conversations about faith matters, we must resort to what Cornelius Plantinga calls summary propositions. The Bible, certainly, uses them: "Biblical authors use such propositions to start an epic ('In the beginning, God created the heavens and the earth'), or to refocus a letter at its midpoint ('God has committed to us the ministry of reconciliation'), or to climax a hymn ('The greatest of these is love'), or to congeal centuries of experience in a proverb ('Pride goes before destruction.'). Biblical authors use summary propositions to do such things all the time. Would it not be perfectly natural for contemporary preachers to follow suit?" [6] We will, then, argue for what Francis Schaeffer called "true truth," not simply personal truth, as important as the latter may sometimes be.

What can be done? It helps to begin with a recognition that

Americans exhibit abysmal ignorance not only of basic theological truths, but of even the value to attend to their beliefs in the first place. Pastors and leaders of religious communities must continue to insist that giving money when the offering plate is passed is not enough. New ways are needed to bring the Bible into our lives in a regular, deep, and meaningful way—and to remind people that reading the Bible is more than a polite exercise. The most cited benefit from respondents' Bible reading is the "closeness" they feel to God after reading (76 percent). That can be encouraged. We need also remind them that they find in the Bible a bracing—and necessary—dose of reality.

> New ways are needed to bring the Bible into our lives in a regular, deep, and meaningful way—and to remind people that reading the Bible is more than a polite exercise.

In surveys, however, people cite a number of roadblocks to Bible reading. Whatever its glorious truths, the Bible looms as an intimidating, hard-to-understand book full of esoteric names and mystifying practices. And of course many people do not read anything in what some call a "postliterate" society. Others cite busyness as a deterrent. Some simply need to be convinced that a book with daunting words and ancient cities and unusual characters can be supremely relevant. And crucial. As with true illiteracy, that is, the inability to read, biblical illiteracy comes with a sense of shame.

Churches and other religious groups will do well to ensure that this lack gets careful attention. It may mean those in the church who have training in the Bible no longer assume a basic familiarity with stories and phrases. We must go slower, start simpler. Writes the Rev. Lillian Daniel, senior minister of the Church of the Redeemer, United Church of Christ, in New Haven, Connecticut:

> *In sermons today I know that before [a passage of] Scripture is read, it is helpful for me to provide an introduction. In the past I would have included extensive historical detail. Today I am careful to mention whether the*

book is in the Old or New Testament, with a
further explanation of what that means. I go
so far as to say, "Since this reading is from the
Old Testament, the story took place long before
Jesus lived."

I do not jump from passage to passage as a
preacher with a biblically literate congregation
can. Instead, I go in depth with one passage,
always retelling the story. . . . I attempt to nur-
ture the familiarity I cannot take for granted." [7]

One of the best and most enduring ways to bring the Bible into our lives is through small groups. As we have noted, four out of ten Americans participate in some kind of small group, most of which are religious in character. Columnist Michael McManus has written: "The one difference I see between churchgoers and those with deep spiritual faith is that the latter meet frequently in small groups with others in fellowship, prayer and mutual support. In this setting people can see the power of prayer and make the exciting discovery that God really cares about them personally." What some churches refer to as "discipling," what others call spiritual direction—pairing one believer with another for the purpose of imparting understanding of biblical truth—has value, as well.

The ways and means will vary—encouraging Bible study groups, ensuring that sermons do more than entertain but creatively teach, leading prospective members to an encounter with a God of truth as well as love—but the goal will remain. Religious groups need to do far more than accumulate members; they must also form followers. Says Leonard Sweet, "People today believe in miracles, in angels. We don't have to argue the case for spiritual realities. . . . Our challenge is to help people believe the right thing."

> Religious groups need to do far more than accumulate members; they must also form followers. Says Leonard Sweet, "People today believe in miracles, in angels. We don't have to argue the case for spiritual realities. . . . Our challenge is to help people believe the right thing."

Formation Focus 2:
Form People in the Soul's Disciplines

To building faith we add also facilitating encounter with God. We know it well in our day: religion must be a matter of the heart, as well as the head. Americans pray and believe in prayer. And they like to feel that they are maturing spiritually, not just emotionally. But if people want to grow spiritually, that does not mean they possess any compelling sense of what that means. They hunger for God's presence but they often feel lax and unschooled. They feel a draw to, in Dallas Willard's phrase, "apprentice" themselves to Christ. Too often, however, they are not given the teaching that would allow them to do more than begin. The return to interest in prayer can be a hopeful sign, though it is not, as Eugene Peterson says, "an automatic good." "It is possible to practice prayer in such a way that it drives us deep into a conniving, calculating egotism. And it is possible to practice prayer in such a way that it bloats us into a prideful ostentation."[8] Clergy often make assumptions about the depth of religious commitment in the lives of their parishioners—that their prayer life is more developed, that they have a fuller knowledge of the Bible and church traditions—than is actually the case. Sometimes clergy themselves, harried and hurried from crushing administrative and pastoral needs, neglect their own prayer life, leaving them with thin personal relationship to the spiritual values they espouse.

> Sometimes clergy themselves, harried and hurried from crushing administrative and pastoral needs, neglect their own prayer life, leaving them with thin personal relationship to the spiritual values they espouse.

Our task of facilitating encounter with God is not made easier by the fact that our culture has lost familiarity with the forming influence of commonly known prayers and psalms and hymns. The Lord's Prayer (or Our Father, as some traditions term it), the Twenty-third Psalm, the stories of the Prodigal Son and Good Samaritan, all once were part of the currency of our common conversation. Now even that influence has waned. We have less of a shared religious vocabulary. The power of tradition has eroded, leaving people more and more attempting to fashion their own spirituality. And if one benefit of our postmodern climate is a greater openness to spiritual, transcendent realities, one drawback is a casual disregard of the value of shared disciplines of formation and contact with the living God in the company of the faithful. Robert Mulholland has a good definition of spiritual formation: "The process of becoming conformed to the image of Christ for the sake of others." [9] We must constantly do battle with the sense that merely individual interpretations, cut loose from the guy wires of tradition and revelation, carry an all-compelling power.

We also face people's perception of a poverty of time. Iin our twenty-four-hour survey, more than half said modern life leaves them "too busy to pray or enjoy God as [they] would like." People want practical, everyday approaches to spiritual life. Prayers on the run, spiritual practices squeezed into the crevices of a busy day have their place. But there is also a key role in training, gaining stamina, learning the practices handed down from centuries of tested wisdom.

This certainly has implications for the home of the twenty-first century. One of the greatest differences between church attenders and those who do not attend is that the churched are more likely to have religious training in the home. They are more likely to have had parents who attended church regularly. Nevertheless, the facts indicate that many parents neglect to model prayer and discuss faith. In the rush to get kids dropped off at school or baseball or ballet practice, have we squeezed out time for nurture? Does the family talk about God? Is the Bible read regularly? Does the family pray together? Churches can do much more to encourage and equip parents in these very tasks.

Such forming of souls requires diligence and practice. It means that twenty-first-century congregations will place priority on prayer over program, presence over practice, authenticity over numbers.

It will also mean attending to the spiritual forming of ministers, just as Catholics have done for centuries. In Protestant seminaries, at least, this development of the soul and cultivating of a transforming relationship to God is often left to the seminarian's own "quiet time."

Seminaries too often emulate the academic goals of the secular academy, neglecting to deepen students' experiences of God's presence. A heady rationalism often substitutes for developing the whole person—heart and soul, not just mind. But, says professor emeritus of spiritual theology James Houston, "We cannot separate prayer from theology, nor theology from prayer. If the triune God is personal and communicative in self-revelation, then prayer is not just one of the disciplines we adopt, as perhaps a substitute for jogging in the morning, but the heart of our faith." We need a systematic, biblical approach to the spiritual life.

Struggling to understand and to love God, Andy Drietcer tells of taking seminary classes from the late priest and spiritual life writer Henri Nouwen. He began to experience, he recounts, "an enduring shift in the question that fueled my intellectual pursuits and my sense of call to ministry. No longer did I ask, 'Does God exist?' Now I began to ask, 'Where do I meet God?'" The answer: "God is greeting me in all parts of my life." Later, in the middle of doctoral studies and adjusting to the advent of children, what Drietcer had studied became reality:

> *In those endless nights [of sleeplessness] something extraordinary happened. As I sat in the cold darkness, wrapped in blankets, a tiny child held to my chest, rocking and softly humming, my times of praying in Henri's course came back to me—but in a new way. I began to imagine that I too was being rocked, held in the arms of God, warm and secure and loved. And who was this in my arms but God's own child, in whose face shone holy light. Each night I sank into this circle of holding divine love and being held by divine love. Each night I beheld the wonder of the*

God of Jesus, the Mystery to which Henri had pointed me. Henri's companionship had prepared me to look at life with new eyes, with a certain attentiveness, with a certain expectation. From this vantage point, I began to see the look, hear the voice, feel the activity of something that just might be the ripples of the presence of God. [10]

Formation Focus 3: Cultivating Virtue

Snapshots of morality in our culture give both cause for concern and hope at the first rays of the new millennium's light.

On the one hand, ethics are in crisis, with little immediate change in sight. A national poll by the Josephson Institute for Ethics in 1998 indicated that dishonesty is rising. It revealed that 47 percent of high school students admitted to stealing from a store in the past year; 70 percent to cheating on an exam; 92 percent to lying to their parents. Barna research shows remarkable similarities of behavior between Christians and non-Christians in matters such as frequency (or infrequency) of donations to nonprofit organizations, tendency to buy a lottery ticket, and incidence of divorce. [11] Religious people in America tend toward a go-along, get-along approach to daily choices. They rarely exemplify the distinctives of what Stanley Hawerwas calls "resident aliens." Congregations in America sometimes fail to provide the distinctive flavor suggested by Jesus calling His followers the salt of the earth. Americans themselves bemoan a perceived loss of moral fiber. Two-thirds of American adults (64 percent) say the country's moral and cultural values have changed for the worse since the 1960s and that society has become too permissive.

On the other hand, there are hopeful, countervailing signs. Gallup polls show that nearly all adults (97 percent) and most teens (69 percent) think honesty is a value that should be taught in public schools to all students. Similar percentages say that teachers should instill "moral courage." And it seems, according to a recent issue of *American Demographics,* that the Millennial Generation (also called Generation Y or Echo Boomers)—those now in elementary, middle, and high schools—are increasingly "retro," even old-fashioned in their dating and mating styles, their attitudes to relationships being more likely to match their grandparents' than the casual approach of their boomer parents. Is part of it the threat of AIDS and other sexually transmitted diseases that make promiscuity physically hazardous? That seems not to account for it all. The *American Demographics* article reported one puzzled boomer sociologist scratching her head and saying, "My twenty-year-old daughter won't live with her boyfriend. . . . She's talking about marrying him." "These kids are fed up with the superficialities of life," reported another article in the same issue. "They have not had a lot of stability in their lives. It's a backlash, a return to tradition and ritual. And that includes marriage. It's all about finding the 'right one'—as opposed to sleeping around." The article went on to suggest that we're "heading for a second coming of family values." [12]

Wendy Shalit's *A Return to Modesty* made considerable news in 1999. In her book, the then twenty-three-year-old author chronicled her attempt to recover traditional values, a search prompted when she heard of "modestyniks"—Orthodox Jewish women who withhold physical contact from men until marriage—while a freshman at Williams College. She found herself fascinated by their allegiance to old ideals, especially amid a sexually saturated contemporary world. Shalit felt amazed at how modestyniks are dismissed as sick by the secular community. Why, she asked, is sexual modesty so threatening to some that they can only respond to it with charges of abuse or delusion? That her book generated considerable media attention and book club selections indicates more than bemused tolerance but rather at least curiosity by the cultural elites.

Both the decline and the reemergence of concern for character suggest work for those in religious communities. Several years ago former Secretary of Education William Bennett's book (and succeeding volumes with similar themes) captured the attention of a nation. *The Book of Virtues* was a surprise publishing phenomenon, no less on college campuses than elsewhere. It included fables, folklore, fiction, drama, and poems by such authors as Aesop, Dickens, Tolstoy, Shakespeare, and Baldwin, to teach virtues, including compassion, courage, honesty, friendship, and faith. The response showed Americans' hunger for instruction in right and wrong.

What can be done? We suggest several strategies:

■ *Encourage those in business and other occupations to talk about the challenges of ethical choices on the job.* Small groups, publications on business ethics, even rallies such as those sponsored by Promise Keepers, can help Americans stay accountable to higher ideals. Small groups that allow frank discussion of ethical issues can help with the living out of such standards.

■ *Help parents reclaim their role as the key to the moral reformation of our culture.* Values are caught as much as taught, and the home environment provides the primary arena for such modeling and shaping. At a time when the church's influence in society wanes, families will need once again to become the heart of moral nurture. "The family will be at the center of the transitions that will create that future," writes George Barna. "As we experience the decentralization of the church in its traditional form, the family will necessarily have to absorb much of the spiritual responsibility that has usually been handled by congregations." [13] But while eight in ten Americans (79 percent) say they received religious training as a child, that number has dropped since the first such measurement in 1952, when it was 94 percent. Part of the answer lies in overcoming parent absenteeism, either from stressed-out, overcommitted parents who leave little time to spend with their children, or from a literal absence. Forty percent of children go to bed each night in homes without a biological father. Don Eberly, former White House aide and founder of the National Fatherhood Initiative, speaks of a "father hunger" in our times. "Father absence," he and Wayne Horn write, "is the most socially destructive problem of our time. American society is in real trouble if we can't reverse this." And the traditional role of motherly nurture must not be lost in Americans' scramble for affluence.

■ *Explore how schools can put character first.* Education specialist Ernest L. Boyer notes how school reform and the pursuit of excellence has often focused only on academics. Public education, however, must also find a place for transmittal (and nurturing) of moral values. He writes:

> Public education must also find a place for transmittal (and nurturing) of moral values.

> *Today, schools are instilling competence in their students—competence in meeting deadlines, gathering information, responding well on tests, and mastering the details of a specialized field. . . . But technical skill, of whatever kind, leaves unanswered some essential questions: Education for what purpose? Competence to what end? . . . The current [school] reform movement should squarely confront the moral obligations of education. . . . During their years of formal learning, students must understand that not all choices are equally valid. They must learn that there is a right and a wrong; that one choice will bring good, another bad.* [14]

This is not, of course, to minimize the complexities of the issue of inculcating moral teaching in our pluralistic day; it is not to say that schools should shoulder the whole burden of moral education; it is to say that we must do more than turn out people who are brilliant but dishonest, skilled but unconstrained by conscience. Much the same can be said about American higher education, as well, an institution that historically has had the task of imparting the essentials of tradition and civilization.

■ *Encourage congregations and their leaders to articulate a clear moral vision.* Only four in ten Americans say they "completely agree" that there are clear guidelines about what is good or evil that apply to everyone regardless of the situation. In our morally relativistic climate, and amid congregations that want to avoid the legalistic excesses of past years, we may need a midcourse correction. The church can and must communicate a stance on moral issues that press upon Americans daily.

■ *Provide a firm yet sympathetic ethical grounding for moral stresses youth face.* A Gallup Youth Survey shows that strong majorities of teens believe that religion offers answers and guidance to some of their thorniest issues, including substance abuse and social issues such as AIDS and abortion. Fifty-four percent said they felt they could find answers in church services, in the Bible, or through talking with clergy when trying to cope with drug and alcohol abuse. In many of these cases, simple availability of clergy and other adult spiritual mentors could go far in helping teens resist peer pressure and destructive activities. Programs such as True Love Waits, through which young people have committed themselves to stay sexually abstinent until marriage, provide support for premarital purity. More than a million teenagers have participated in making the pledge, usually done in a public ceremony.

■ *Invest in the lives of children in direct, hands-on ways:* mentoring, adoption, volunteering at schools, home schooling, teaching Sunday School, working as a teacher or teacher's aide. Most people's basic values "gel" by the time they reach age twenty. Much needs to be done to target children before then. Everyone who has children, and those who don't, should ask, "Are there ways I should help pass along values and faith to the next generation?" Insight delivered at a distance through youth-group talks and sermons needs flesh-and-blood immediacy.

Formation Focus 4:
Target Age Groups with Sensitivity

With more people living longer, we now face increasing numbers of generations alive at the same time. Lengthening life spans mean that five generations (soon more) of a family may exist at once. Even more significant is increasing segmentation, even fragmentation. The "generation gap" of the sixties and seventies will have nothing on what is to come. And the number of age-related subcultures is rising. As one writer notes, "The Boomers had the hippies, folkies, and yippies (politicized hippies). By my count, in emerging generations there are about a dozen major *categories* of subcultures, each with multiple 'tribes.' These subcultures cluster around such activities, issues, and values as extreme sports, arts, political causes, environmentalism/animal rights, alternative sexuality and gender practices, technology, economics, music style and fashion, racial and ethnic status, and protecting/respecting historical beliefs." [15]

> The "generation gap" of the sixties and seventies will have nothing on what is to come. And the number of age-related subcultures is rising.

Many church leaders now ask what it means to minister in such times. Often Generation Xers are particularly targeted for specialized ministry. Besides, this young generation is the first generation of "latchkey" kids (those left at home unsupervised while both parents worked). They were affected by rising divorce rates and fractured homes. TV was a constant. Observes Richard Kew, "If the question that Boomers asked during their choppy transition to adulthood was 'What does it all mean?' I would suggest the question many Xers ask (which is then projected into their culture) is, 'Is there anyone who is there for me?'" Perhaps Gen Xer Tom Beaudoin expressed the challenge best when he wrote in *Virtual Faith*, "During our lifetimes, especially during the critical period of the 1980s, pop culture was the amniotic fluid that sustained us. For a generation of kids who had a fragmented or completely broken relationship to 'formal' or 'institutional' religion, pop culture filled the spiritual gaps." It was the young's surrogate clergy because "popular religion usurped the role institutional clergy played for previous generations." [16] Popular culture becomes the universal reference, a new sign of community.

Can we learn how to communicate cross-generationally? Will a "one-size-fits-all" approach to nurturing faith work amid the growing segmentation of age cohorts? Will we learn to pass along our faith to young people, many of whom already feel alienated and marginalized from mainstream culture and traditional religious communities? Will we capitalize on the incredibly powerful spiritual search of the young?

> George Barna has found that more than two-thirds of all adults who have accepted Christ as their Savior made their decision to do so before the age of eighteen.

George Barna has found that more than two-thirds of all adults who have accepted Christ as their Savior made their decision to do so before the age of eighteen. The times of transition and accelerated change we will face in coming years will only accentuate differences between generational groups, only make more urgent the need to reach the young and support all age groups.

Experts debate generational names, but here is one way to think of it:

- GIs (born 1901–1924)
- Silent Generation (1925–1942) (These two are sometimes lumped together and called "Builders.")
- Boomers (1946–1964)
- Busters or Gen Xers (1965–1981)
- Blasters or Millennials (1982–2003)

The question confronting the church in the opening years of a new millennium is what does this increasing age stage fragmentation mean? We believe the jury is out. One way the debate is sometimes framed is shown in a pair of articles that recently appeared in *Leadership,* a journal for pastors.

In the article titled, "Two Pastors in a Demographic Debate: Should the Church Target Generations?" each church leader took a different view. First, James Emery White answered, "Yes, so that all may know." His argument: "Targeting [a particular age group] is not the refusal to take the gospel to the whole world. Nor is it ignoring the diverse range of generations within the church. Instead, it is acknowledging the characteristics of the place where your church resides and developing your outreach accordingly. As a Texas pastor said to me, 'We target baby boomers because that is Plano [Texas]. To neglect targeting this group would be to deny the reality of our mission field.'" [17] With this in mind, many churches are launching a specifically Gen X worship service, often on Saturday nights, usually with contemporary music.

Then Garth Bolinder, a pastor pushing a more broad-based strategy argued otherwise: "Our high school students usually meet in small groups on Sunday evening," he said. "[One] night they joined the adults. These students are younger than busters—call them the 'millennium generation' if you want. Did they sit in the back of the sanctuary in their grunge clothes and talk about the latest episode of 'Friends'? No way! They were up front, praying aloud with fervency and feeling, seeking their Heavenly Father in heartfelt prayer. Many adults were moved to tears and silence as they listened. Jesus promised that he would be present when two or three gathered in his name. I wonder if he was talking about individuals or generations?" [18]

What is the answer? Clearly, the millennial generation will form unique (as well as shared) values, beliefs, and attitudes about relationships. They will create their own culture, much as did young people in the 1960s. So do and so will other generations. If sensitive to the opportunity, if willing to learn to speak in new forms and with emerging media, the church can help all ages shape their values and beliefs, grounding them in Christian truth, not vague spiritual feelings or syncretistic mix-and-match amalgams.

Doing so may require thinking outside the normal boundaries. Reaching younger age groups may mean attempting some new strategies. Michael Slaughter, a United Methodist pastor in Ohio, became troubled by the recognition that twentysomethings are largely absent from worship services. How could he reach them? In 1995, he says, the church got serious about attracting them. "Prior to this time we assumed that the same contemporary worship style that was effective in reaching the unchurched Boomer would also be effective in reaching the Buster. Wrong assumption! The children of Boomers have very different felt needs." He and his staff listened (through research, surveys, and visiting other churches) and developed a strategy. In their case, they brought a staff person who would build a team to offer a targeted Gen X service. After six months, attendance was averaging around three hundred for worship with "Stage 2" Bible studies offered afterward. [19]

Formation Focus 5: Communicate with Sanctified Creativity

As rising generations drive some congregations to target age groups, they will also require more creativity in communicating faith to an increasingly diverse culture. Ours is a culture that no longer turns first for information or motivation to a written word or "talking head" lecture. Consider: we live in a country in which 99.9 percent of households have televisions and 97 percent have plumbing. Few aspects of American life are more universal than TV. "*See* not *read* is the word for this generation," says Michael Slaughter. [20] An average child will have watched five thousand hours of television by age five. Children now are born into a culture saturated with visual and sonic media. Young children are vastly more conversant about characters on *Sesame Street* than those in the Bible, older children more concerned about the latest CD than what goes on at church. In a typical week 38 percent of Gen Xers watch MTV. [21] Young people of all ages are as likely to take their cues about what to think or wear or feel from TV commercials as from church or parents. Commentators now talk of the rise of television as the primary medium for politics. In the modern world, says Leonard Sweet, culture's primary tool of communication was the word. Now, in postmodern times, he suggests, it is the image.

Our twenty-four-hour survey, not surprisingly, showed that television and radio media have significant impact on American believers—

and certainly adults. A quarter (24 percent) told us that they had watched or listened to a religiously oriented television or radio program within the past twenty-four hours—considerably more than had been to a Bible study or prayer group (15 percent). Christians, interestingly, are known as people of the Book. But what if fewer people gain most of their information from a book of any kind? If the trend continues toward more interactivity, away from printed words and merely spoken words, what might it mean for the church's efforts to communicate its faith? In an age when "surround sound" systems grace living rooms and video screens get larger and more "in your face," in a time when people are increasingly "plugged in" and conditioned to see choreographed, well-produced motion, does the church need to adapt? One commentator, Terry Teachout, writes in *The Wall Street Journal* that, novels have given way to movies as the shapers of "national conversation." It used to be that people talked about novels in daily conversation. Now it's movies. "Many young American story tellers who once might have chosen to write novels are instead making small-scale movies of considerable artistic merit," he writes. [22] Will the church of the emerging millennium need to become more savvy in such arts?

We suggest several ways a sanctified creativity might respond to the changing needs of rising generations:

■ *Rediscover and reclaim the role of artistic expression in worship, ministry, and witness.* Our culture is not only high tech, it is high touch. People are interested in experiences that engage all their senses. Historically the church often was patron to great pieces of music and art, from Bach chorales to the Sistine Chapel. Church leaders need to discover new ways in which the church in the twenty-first century can encourage artistic expression and the use of the arts to express faith, worship, to witness to what we know and believe. How can the church encourage and sponsor new forms of poetry, music, mime, drama, cinema, theater?

One reason such questions matter is that people increasingly expect experiences (including those of worship) to be interactive. How can worship be more than occupying a pew and hearing someone talk? How can it become digitized? We predict that more and more churches will use visual media—Powerpoint, slide presentations, drama—to complement the auditory experience of music and hearing the spoken word. A multisensory approach to worship may bear fruit, where everything in the service—architecture, lighting, banners, songs, prayer, fellowship, even the smells—contribute. Is this perhaps why some are rediscovering more liturgical worship, with its incense, candles, and historic Christian rituals?

■ *Reclaim the value of telling the story.* Sermons and other forms of religious communication continue to be largely didactic and conceptual. The culture, on the other hand, grows more and more hungry for stories. "We live, for good or ill," writes Patricia Hampl, "in an autobiographical age. The memoir practically nudges the novel off the book-review pages." [23] The Judeo-Christian message, it should be noted, has always been grounded in history—His story:

> Sermons and other forms of religious communication continue to be largely didactic and conceptual. The culture, on the other hand, grows more and more hungry for stories.

> *Then you shall declare before the LORD your God: "My father was a wandering Aramean, and he went down into Egypt with a few people and lived there and became a great nation, powerful and numerous. But the Egyptians mistreated us and made us suffer, putting us to hard labor. Then we cried out to the LORD, the God of our fathers, and the LORD heard our voice and saw our misery, toil and oppression. So the LORD brought us out of Egypt with a mighty hand and an outstretched arm, with great terror and with miraculous signs and*

wonders. He brought us to this place and gave us this land, a land flowing with milk and honey" (Deuteronomy 26:5-9).

And of course, when pressed to a nutshell presentation of the good news of Christ, the Apostle Paul told a story: "For what I received I passed on to you as of first importance: that Christ died for our sins according to the Scriptures, that he was buried, that he was raised on the third day according to the Scriptures, and that he appeared to Peter, and then to the Twelve" (1 Corinthians 15:3-5).

Sermons and other forms of communication need to be soaked, then, in the Great Story. But increasingly important to allowing truth to "take" in the postmodern consciousness will require incorporating the preacher's own experiences, and the lived experiences of others. And such stories, when they become a vehicle for conveying truth in sermons and other writings, should avoid being too tidy, too moralistic. To some extent, the story itself, told well, conveys truth and reality. And the way in which our entertainment media have moved may also suggest some strategies for communicating: in contrast to the linear story lines of "Father Knows Best" or "Leave It to Beaver," which clearly and satisfyingly found resolution, now TV programs are more episodic, evocative, less concerned about the resolution or moral and more concerned about the effect. "Laugh-in," with its potpourri approach, or "MASH," with its layering of story on story, and especially "ER" demonstrate the shift.

Indeed, young people will increasingly shy away from lectures or monologues. They want to participate in the discovery of truth, not simply be presented with it in finished form. Churches that experiment with dialogical sermons or more interactive classes often find an end result of greater effectiveness and more resonance from the young.

■ *Harness the Web and Internet.* The so-called Information Marketplace has made a deep impact on this generation. The Internet, what *The Wall Street Journal* recently termed "spirituality's controversial new frontier," is only beginning to shape perceptions and experiences of community. Writes Lisa Miller, "Plug 'God' into a Netscape search, and you'll get as many as 600,000 responses, remarkably close to the 775,000 sites devoted to 'sex.' Yahoo! Inc. lists 17,000 sites devoted to religion and spirituality, compared with 12,000 about movies and 600 about home and garden. . . . Nearly every traditional denomination now has a Web site, as do a fast-growing number of individual churches, mosques, and synagogues." [24] When publishing company Christianity Today, Inc. linked with America Online to create Christianity Online, an array of chat rooms, online periodicals, and Web site links, it became one of AOL's most popular features. And users were interested in more than information and news. John LaRue, one of Christianity Today, Inc.'s vice presidents, notes that subscribers wanted to employ the site's potential for community, flocking to chat rooms and prayer request bulletin boards.

> As our twenty-four-hour survey shows, the percentage of those who turn to the World Wide Web for daily spiritual sustenance is modest (2 to 3 percent). But if the phenomenal growth of that medium is any indication, the future will see major changes.

As our twenty-four-hour survey shows, the percentage of those who turned to the World Wide Web for daily spiritual sustenance was modest (2 to 3 percent). But if the phenomenal growth of that medium is any indication, the future will see major changes. Indeed, a survey with a younger age cohort would have returned vastly different results. The rising number of computer-savvy younger generations, some of whom hit the Internet first thing on awaking and visit chat rooms into wee hours, will change how we communicate. Such technology will give us new opportunities to do our work and ministry, while at the same time competing with what we offer. How can the church harness technology without being ruled by it? The head of MIT's Laboratory for Computer Science says that the Web is "ideally suited for spreading the word; the ability of each church to reach hundreds of millions of people with information about their beliefs and functions will widen the possibilities for affiliation." [25]

Efficiency alone, however, is not enough. For all this impressive efficiency, people will still want human contact. There is a two-dimensionality to online reality. It is virtual, but not actual, reality. One father worries about his "net surfer" son, who seems to have more friends whom he knows only online than he does in person in his immediate community. He constantly "talks" with them through e-mail and piggybacked chat rooms and instant messages. But the need for actual, not virtual community will never go away. The longing for flesh-and-blood encounter with real people will never eradicate the need for face-to-face encounters through Bible study groups, church, and informal meetings with others of like spiritual mind.

For all this impressive efficiency, people will still want human contact. There is a two-dimensionality to online reality. It is virtual, but not actual, reality.

■ *Use surveys and other tools to listen to the emerging needs of our culture and varied subcultures.* Tools, such as Pantego Bible Church's Christian Life Profile, can help churches and other groups to not only listen, but to measure effectiveness in conveying a message. When Rick Warren began Saddleback Community Church in Orange County, California, in the 1970s, he discovered through communitywide surveys that high-quality nursery care and sermons that stressed relevancy to daily life were key factors in community residents' choice of a church. A simple thing, in a way, but one to which he and his congregation could easily respond, to great effect, and with deeper fruit in lives touched with the Gospel.

Congregations will do well to stay close to their people's needs and lacks and hopes through constant listening. Surveys can query: To what extent do people put their faith into action? What are the physical and spiritual needs of the people the church is supposed to serve? What is bringing people to church—and keeping them away?

Congregations will do well to stay close to their people's needs and lacks and hopes through constant listening.

The focus in the years to come must not turn inward only, of course. More waits to be done than working spirituality down deep. A wider culture needs winsome, persuasive, sensitive invitations to experience the life that believers share with one another. The next chapter explores how that can happen.

WHERE SHOULD WE GO?: REACHING BEYOND OUR WALLS

"If we want our friends to consider seriously our gospel message, we must depend upon more than intellectual argument. . . . We must rouse them from their settled complacency as we depend on the Holy Spirit to shine out through all the various lamps of good works we can possibly raise to the glory of our Father."

—JOHN STACKHOUSE [1]

IN ONE OF Nashville's affluent suburbs, Saint Bartholomew's Episcopal Church occupies a hollowed-out knoll surrounded by oak- and hackberry-wooded hills and upscale homes. Its sanctuary, a kind of contemporary ark of brick and stained glass, towers above a grassy field that hosts church picnics and community soccer games. From the outside, a visitor would be hard-pressed to say what was different about this church from its other suburban counterparts. But on a Sunday morning one will occasionally hear another sound along with organ-accompanied hymns and guitar-backed praise songs: Sudanese Christians playing instruments made resonant from stretched animal skins and drums carved from logs, singing to the swaying rhythms of African beats and world harmonies, leading congregants in praise in an African dialect.

The presence of Sudanese refugees in the services of a denomination known for its dignified climate comes as no accident. Several years ago, members of the parish's Great Commission Commission began meeting with other Nashville church leaders interested in missions. "Nashville to the Nations," as the group was called, brought together pastors and other lay mission leaders to pray and strategize ways to increase mission mindedness. Not long after, a member of Saint Bartholomew's, Susan Crane, a fiftysomething woman fluent in two languages, discovered that a number of Sudanese refugees lived in Nashville and more were on the way. Crane learned that they were part of the same Anglican (Episcopal) tradition as Saint Bartholomew's.

Then Crane and others met Dominic, a transplanted Sudanese, and invited him to attend. He came, and came back, bringing his brother and later, other Sudanese friends. "Our church had been praying for two years," recalls one member of the church, "asking God to show us an unreached people He wanted us to be involved with." "Finally it dawned on us," says Crane: "this was the group God wanted us to minister to. He was bringing the group to us."

Members and friends of Saint B's (as members nickname their church) got more involved. Included among the volunteers was Joyce Shepard, an articulate assistant to a Nashville publisher of Civil War books. Shepard brought her newfound concern for the Sudanese to an adult Sunday School class, which began collecting money for bicycles for pastors in Sudan to aid them in their pastoral rounds. At the same time, more and more Sudanese made their way to Saint B's, finding a warm welcome, perhaps in part due to a divine impression spoken out loud years earlier, a prophetic word, many called it, that the church was to become a center for many nations.

Opportunities to assist the transplanted people mushroomed.

More and more members felt called to help. The Sudanese families needed help with paying rent, finding transportation, filling out forms. One man's wife, left behind in Sudan, desperately needed money for chemotherapy. The money arrived a week too late; it was used instead for her funeral expenses. The women of the church threw a baby shower for one pregnant Sudanese woman. One family took on sponsorship of a newly transplanted family. Volunteers taxied Sudanese young people to the church's youth group, where some made decisions for a saving faith in Christ. Members helped one Sudanese woman launch a Bible study for women, though it sputtered and soon was discontinued. Joyce Shepard became a part-time staff person to work in Sudanese ministries. Members from Saint B's accompanied Sudanese on trips back to Uganda and Sudan to learn ways to help.

But the ministry was far from one-sided. The Sudanese bring a vigor to worship (evidenced by the African anthems they occasionally sing in services) and a depth that comes from suffering and facing martyrdom. Says Saint B's rector, Michael Ellis, "American Christians often live without a clear view of Christianity in other places in the world. We think right here is the only place things are happening. But the Sudanese have brought us face-to-face with deep faith. Yes, they need healing for what they have endured, and we help them in one sense, of course, but they build *our* faith and challenge *our* commitment. We get to rub shoulders with people who possess a radiant testimony to the power of faith. This has given us more than a glimpse of a God at work throughout the world, a God doing things elsewhere sometimes more profoundly than right here. And while they work on their own issues of reconciliation and forgiveness related to the bloodshed of their land, we are reminded of our own need for racial reconciliation in our setting."

The experience of Saint B's is being repeated across the country, not in an avalanche of congregations, but nevertheless in significant numbers. Indeed, the story of their being catapulted into ministry illustrates trends in outreach sure to shape the vitality of American religious organizations and churches in Millennium Three. How can believers serve and witness as a

> How can believers serve and witness as a partner to God's purposes in the coming world, fully engaged in reaching out to the hurting and needy, seeking new models to tackle societal problems, inviting others to share in the transforming life God makes possible?

partner to God's purposes in the coming world, fully engaged in reaching out to the hurting and needy, seeking new models to tackle societal problems, inviting others to share in the transforming life God makes possible? We identify here four patterns sure to affect ways we can and will do our work beyond our walls.

Outreach Mandate 1: Think Globally

While worldwide political fragmentation and tribalism rise, while wars in Eastern Europe and Indonesia and Africa heat up, in another sense international boundaries are fading. We drink coffee with the help of four states and six foreign companies. Multinational corporations plant offices across vast language and geographical boundaries. Recognition of brands like Coke and Nike becomes increasingly universal. We travel thousands of miles in mere hours. "Far off" is "right here"; in our increasingly webbed and connected world, we communicate half a world away in seconds. And America itself grows more visibly pluralistic with world cultures and ethnic diversity next door.

> We travel thousands of miles in mere hours. "Far off" is "right here"; in our increasingly webbed and connected world, we communicate half a world away in seconds. And America itself grows more visibly pluralistic with world cultures and ethnic diversity next door.

Writes Tom Sine, "We are hardwiring our planet electronically into a single global system of satellites, fax machines, and Internet communications. Borders are melting." [2] The extent of this globalization defies precedent. The potential benefits are immense, just as are the enormous perils, the great potential for misuse of information and power.

Some argue that "representative Christianity" in the twenty-first century will look less like that of Europe or North America and more like that of Africa, Asia, and Latin America. Fervent faith is changing the profile of these continents, and their faith and understandings of following Christ will release new insights when transported here. Christianity there is spreading at the same unprecedented rate that it shows decline in the West. Our own cultural expression of faith will lack fullness without this global richness.

The new globalization also holds huge promise for groups ready to "go into all the world," as Jesus summoned His followers. There are notable exceptions, of course, but less and less do national borders throw up walls or dictate isolation. It is no wonder that short-term mission trips have increased dramatically in recent years; we are more aware of other cultures, see distances as less of a barrier, and have technology at our fingertips to reach them as never before. Translators for Wycliffe Bible Translators, to cite an example from traditional missionary work, "are now able to produce the first draft translation of a Bible book into a related dialect with a computer program instead of additional linguists." [3] Far-flung missionaries have been some of the first to take advantage of the worldwide scope of the Internet to trade ministry tips, update financial contributors, and build virtual communities with those who lend spiritual and emotional support. Anyone with access to a computer and a modem can now have at the fingertips astonishing amounts of information about other countries, other peoples, and ways to navigate through new cultures.

This new power through information technology means that the new poor are not simply those economically deprived, but those who lack connections—electronically. Access to information will more and more determine survival and success. Leonard Sweet calls what we are witnessing a growing gap between the knows and the know-nots. The church can play a part in helping to build bridges, perhaps adding to its traditional tutoring programs tutoring in computer literacy.

And the influx of many cultures to our shores means that the "mission field" in many communities has already arrived next door.

> Access to information will more and more determine survival and success. Leonard Sweet calls what we witness a growing gap between the knows and the know-nots.

> The influx of many cultures to our shores means that the "mission field" in many communities has already arrived next door.

Nashville's flourishing Sudanese population will be a story played out again and again. As new people groups inhabit our towns and cities, will they hear an invitation to friendship and, when trust is built, a sharing of faith? Much of the spread of the Christian message will depend on the answer.

Outreach Mandate 2: Act Locally

If, with the advent of technology, come new opportunities for global communication, so also do changing demographics mean new opportunities locally.

We have already seen the burgeoning interest in spirituality sweeping much of our culture; we have seen how Americans routinely discuss spiritual matters at work, with neighbors, with family. More than half said that in the past twenty-four hours they had talked "to someone about God or some aspect of . . . faith or spirituality." A full quarter said they had counseled someone "from a spiritual perspective."

Most of Americans' words of witness and acts of service take place in their daily settings. Not all need be urged to set up mission outposts in Borneo; indeed, in our times of information overload, when images pour forth from news magazines and TV screens of global suffering on an epic scale, people may need to be encouraged to do the thing within reach. They can be equipped to share their faith with their friends and neighbors with simple training in what many call friendship evangelism (see more about this later). Many can be encouraged to volunteer at efforts to help the homeless or counsel the addicted within driving distance. Congregations can develop new partnerships with other organizations to bring social health to their community. And more can be done to encourage "sister church" programs where a more affluent church reaches out to a less affluent one—coming together not only in worship services but in small groups, as well as choir exchanges, and the leaders of the churches exchanging preachers from time to time. These local expressions allow hands-on help and accessible opportunities.

One demographic change may make this local emphasis even more feasible. More than half the world's population live in cities; almost four hundred cities worldwide support a population of one million or more. Cities in the U.S. continue to swell. But the urban renaissance has to do with more than people who have no choice but to endure crowding and sprawl. Some observers believe that the decades-long trend of urban flight is reversing. Cities have become magnets once again for art, entertainment, fine restaurants, community development, and trendy apartments. Much of this represents affluent professionals opting for convenience and easy access to urban culture. But some of these urban enclaves also play host to people genuinely interested in spiritual things. And some have a conscience that can be prodded to do more. They can be encouraged to offer simple help to someone they can see or easily find with an agency or church's assistance.

One social observer writes: "Inner-city youngsters, especially, live in an atmosphere that says, 'You can't make it.' The messages they receive are relentlessly negative. The youngsters have a particular need for mature adults who can take them aside, give them a hug, and tell them, quietly and gently, an entirely different story." 4 Why can't more believers, whether they inhabit suburban, rural, or urban areas, be awakened to the possibilities? That this is happening may already be seen in a trend toward hands-on contact between the privileged and the underprivileged, including mentoring and face-to-face volunteering programs. At the same time, however, our society's increasing fragmentation works against such crossing of boundaries. And suburbanites are largely terrified of (or just plain indifferent to) inner cities. Still, churches will be focal in the recovery of societal health.

Outreach Mandate 3:
Reach Out Evangelistically

When Gallup survey takers tested an initial draft of the twenty-four-hour survey, we observed a fascinating phenomenon: a fair number of those called, when told that survey questions would focus on spiritual life, bristled or grew defensive. We ended up starting out with less spiritually focused questions, realizing that many feel tender or vulnerable on matters of faith and spiritual practice. The feelings we uncovered point to ongoing challenges of making faith known in our postmodern, largely post-Christian era.

Recently a friend of one of the authors was browsing through a Barnes & Noble bookstore with a friend. They struck up a conversation with the store manager. "Halfway through our conversation," the friend recounted, "I told him we were both pastors." The manager registered shock at how cordial the conversation had been. "I normally only hear from Christians when they are mad," he said. As the three sat down at the coffee bar, the manager recounted stories of religious people who had called, written, or walked in the store to say they would never do business there; they contacted him only to protest Halloween displays or objectionable books.

Believers in Christian faith have some bridge-building to do in the century to come; too often the message of religious people has seemed only judgmental and less than inviting or redemptive. At least some of the muting of a Christian cultural voice has to do with the manner in which faith is communicated. Believers need greater sensitivity than ever before.

More than ever, the burden of proof on a communicator of spiritual truth is not whether God exists or that religions have valuable insights; it is rather that there can possibly be a set of beliefs that could be compellingly, universally true. Apologetics, that field that seeks to make faith convincing, no longer needs to focus so much on whether God exists, but whether God can be *known,* whether truth can be found. Further, writes John Stackhouse of Regent College, "Too much of our Christian witness today concentrates on trying to convince people that Christianity is true. We need instead to consider [first] two prior problems. First, most

> Apologetics, that field that seeks to make faith convincing, no longer needs to focus so much on whether God exists, but whether God can be *known,* whether truth can be found.

Americans . . . are ignorant of even the basics of authentic Christian faith. And second, most people think that they do understand Christianity and thus feel entitled to dismiss it out of hand." More than convincing people in our postmodern times that such beliefs are true, he argues, we must first establish that they are plausible. [5]

Christians forget that so much of their in-house vocabulary (words like *redemption, sanctification, atonement)* fall on modern secular ears like a foreign language, increasingly so in our biblically illiterate culture. Or believers assume that a quote from Scripture can clinch an argument; in reality most Americans have little sense of either the content or authority of the Bible. Indeed, trying to persuade someone with the argument that "the Bible said it, that settles it, I believe it" may increasingly ring hollow.

Instead, people in the coming century will look for a faith made real in daily life and experience and choices. More is needed than urgent words; postmoderns insist on authenticity; faith sharing must grow out of a larger life and witness. Its claims to truth must be buttressed with a changed life, with an experienced and personally felt faith.

The institutional church has failed to some extent on this score. The loss of church members in most Christian denominations in recent decades can be traced in part to lack of intentional (and informed) evangelism. Some denominations that have launched emphases such as a Decade of Evangelism continue to hemorrhage members. One observer, commenting on evangelism among his fellow Episcopalians, said, "We've lost the ability to care that people don't know Jesus Christ." A lack of urgency combined with a kind sensitivity has left many congregations and religious institutions in crisis.

On the other hand, one of the key signs of a vital church and an authentic personal faith is energy and urgency to share the good things being discovered. Evangelism, sometimes called the "e-word" in mainline denominational circles from distaste of earlier revivalistic excesses, can be renovated. For the church to continue its witness, evangelism must be reclaimed. Especially when it is approached in a way that is winsome and nonthreatening. Those involved in evangelism can point out that a vital faith and church participation can help in daily life in these ways:

■ *In dealing with the problems of life.* Surveys continually show that the religiously involved are often more able to cope with life's stresses and daily problems than those who are not. Among our "saints among us" survey, we found that the highly spiritually committed registered measurably greater happiness.

■ *In strengthening the religious and moral development of their children.* Most parents put a high premium on the religious nurture of their children. Most realize that moral and spiritual development will not take place in a vacuum.

■ *In helping to understand the meaning of life.* Surveys show people searching with new intensity for a deeper dimension to their lives. Most of our twenty-four-hour survey respondents said they lived by a philosophy of life or set of rules. But that they also said they felt a need in their lives for spiritual growth demonstrates a search for even deeper foundations.

■ *In enriching one's sense of community and support.* Many of the unchurched have active spiritual lives and pray regularly, but those involved in evangelizing can point out that a prayer life thrives only in the company of others. Growing faith needs a corporate context through prayer meetings, small groups, corporate worship, and regular contact with like-minded believers. Evangelism, then, will not only present the saving message of new life in Christ; it will also issue forth in an invitation to a new community.

In the coming decades, often the only thing to stand between an unchurched person and a house of worship will be a simple invitation, as seen in the results of a study on the reasons people currently join a church (with the option given of answering with more than one response):

> In the coming decades, often the only thing to stand between an unchurched person and a house of worship will be a simple invitation, as seen in the results of a study on the reasons people currently join a church.

- Those who come because of the Sunday School: 3 to 6 percent
- Those who walk in of their own initiative: 3 to 8 percent
- Those who come because of the activities: 4 to 10 percent
- Those who come because of a particular minister: 10 to 20 percent
- Those who come because of an evangelistic program: 10 to 20 percent
- Those who come at the invitation of a friend or relative: 60 to 80 percent

A number of churches across the country (indeed, the world) have found programs that help with the kinds of approaches to evangelism we have discussed. One of those is called Alpha.

Alpha began two decades ago, when Charles Marnham, a clergyman at Holy Trinity Brompton, London, began looking for a means of presenting the basic principles of the Christian faith to new Christians in a relaxed and informal setting. The talks that became integral to the course addressed such fundamental questions as "Who is Jesus?" "How and why do I pray?" and "How does God guide us?" By the time Nicky Gumbel took over Alpha in 1990, the course was a central feature of the church's life, with the number of participants regularly totaling around 100 people in each course.

It was while leading his second Alpha course that Nicky made a discovery that transformed the church's whole approach to the program. As he looked around at the thirteen members of his small group, he realized with a start that apart from the three Christian helpers, the other ten members of the group were nonchurchgoers.

Here is what happened:

> *"They had all the normal objections: 'What about other religions?' 'What about suffering?' and so on, and we had a stormy first six weeks," [Nicky Gumbel] said. Then they went away on the "Holy Spirit weekend" and all ten announced their Christian conversion.*
>
> *The experience transformed Nicky's thinking about Alpha. He realized how this simple course in basic Christianity could become a powerful medium for evangelism. He quickly worked to give the course the kind of "feel" that would be particularly attractive to nonchurchgoers. The method of welcome, the atmosphere of the small groups, the food, the seating, the flowers, the sound, and the material of the talks themselves were all changed to make them as attractive as possible to the person who walked in "off the street." . . . [No] question should be treated as too trivial, threatening or illogical. Every question would be addressed courteously and thoughtfully—and none would ever be "pestered" if they chose not to continue with the course. [Says Gumbel,] "A lot of people live their lives without anybody listening to them very much. But when they come to the Alpha course suddenly they discover that people are interested in what they've got to say. Alpha, just by its structure, empowers people who often have very little power or freedom in their lives." [6]*

More than one million people have participated in this program in the last five years. It provides an entry program to the church, and is scoring major successes because it is both embracing of all comers, and yet presents the Gospel lucidly and powerfully. It is but one example of the kind of creative, sensitive thrusts an evangelistic agenda will require in the coming years. An example not necessarily to be cloned, but to be seen as a model for the possibilities just waiting for sanctified creativity.

Many people, surveys reveal, live lives in great need of spiritual guidance and divine comfort. They have questions about making sense of their lives and their suffering; they wonder if they are truly loved by God; they worry that they have so failed at their lives that they lie beyond the reach of God's grace. For many such individuals, a simple invitation, a kind ear, a clear exposition of faith, will make a universe of difference, and hold eternal repercussions.

Outreach Mandate 4: Live Compassionately

History offers plenty of examples in which faith does not always end in compassion. In one period late in the nineteenth-century South, for example, the number of lynchings of blacks rose right alongside the number of evangelistic revivals. But the ideals of religious institutions, at their best, insist on compassion. One 1988 Gallup survey found that the closer people feel to God, the better they feel about themselves and other people. Our twenty-four-hour survey confirmed this faith-compassion connection.

> One 1988 Gallup survey found that the closer people feel to God, the better they feel about themselves and other people.

"During the last twenty-four hours," we asked, "was there an occasion when you went out of your way to help someone else because of spiritual or faith reasons?" As we reported, not quite half (45 percent) said yes. And missionaries and evangelists have for centuries demonstrated the genuineness of their concern and authenticity of their message through acts of compassion. Indeed, compassion is to be a hallmark of the believer. People of faith are called to care for those whom Jesus called "the least of these" (Matthew 25:40) and those on the outside will increasingly expect consonance of word and act, creed and deed. It is no accident that Mother Teresa of Calcutta repeatedly emerged in surveys as the most admired woman in the world; who has better demonstrated such radical compassion?

For her, faith was no escape, but a prod to action and a spur to prayer. Says African-American professor of preaching William Pannell of Fuller Theological Seminary, "The church must recapture some of the glory days of spirituality when those in the forefront of social transformation were arguing most passionately for holiness and the disciplines associated with spiritual renewal." One thinks of medieval monasteries that provided refuge and physical nourishment; the nineteenth-century work of William Wilberforce campaigning against slavery in England; the Salvation Army, which offered a place to eat and sleep along with a Gospel message; Dorothy Day and her Catholic Worker Movement; or the Rev. Martin Luther King, Jr., whose identity as both a minister and the most tireless worker for civil rights was not coincidental.

As the needs of our world grow with a global population just crossing the six billion threshold, the church will need to become more fully engaged in helping the hurting. To do so will mean not only providing a safe haven for the comfortable and the long-time attender, but encouraging its members to move out of their comfort zones and reach people on the margins of society, as Jesus called us to do. Some say that there are more than 2,500 verses in the Bible just on the poor, to say nothing of other pressing social needs. The work to be done looms large. Some will be called to donate time and money. Others will address the larger systemic issues of a society that allows disparity and ignores need.

Some conclude there is no use, however. Many congregational and community leaders report "compassion fatigue," the sense that people cannot give more—or give at all. We see no reason for compassion fatigue to decline, not with the constant influx of images and news from every global quarter. But the pressing physical needs of our cities and towns and rural areas can provide a simple starting place for many people. And a wholistic response to the world's problems will stress that acts of kindness and sharing compassion do not come as options of faith, but indispensable expressions of it."If one of you says to [a poor person]," we hear in Scripture, "'Go, I wish you well; keep warm and well fed,' but does nothing about his physical needs, what good is it? In the same way, faith by itself, if it is not accompanied by action, is dead" (James 2:16-17).

Such tasks, we might add, are not only accomplished individually, but best done in partnership. There is strength in association, as Saint Bartholomew's discovered with its Sudanese ministry, linking with partners locally and even around the world, bringing in speakers from other settings who had worked with Sudanese. A cord of three strands is not quickly broken, the writer of Ecclesiastes reminds us.

A group of churches and agencies in Fresno, California, has discovered the power of linking hands. The originators of the program of remarkable cooperation say that by coming together as groups with spiritual aims they have been able to stem the "turf war" syndrome that dominates so many communities and prevents cooperation among nonprofit institutions, including churches. They have formed a roundtable monthly discussion group among thirteen churches and religiously oriented agencies to share needs and resources. They say of this idea, "It is our job to reflect on what God is doing and to join God where He is at work!" This theological perspective reflects more trust in God working through His body, and not just through some elite group of individuals.

The leaders of the Fresno interdenominational group have found that the single most significant problem in their city is the "disconnection"—alienation—between people and the groups with the human, material, and financial resources needed to help them build healthy communities. Can inner-city youth be rescued from lives of desperation and crime? Can the homeless be given more than just a meal but also help for a fresh start in life? Until recently the answers were in doubt. But today, thanks to the inspired leadership of courageous and compassionate individuals, as well as new, creative partnerships between faith communities and other groups, the answer is more hopeful.

Faith provides just the kind of impetus and staying power to keep people giving and working for good. Pity or guilt or anguish over the state of things may prompt some acts of mercy but it will ultimately be faith that keeps the lamps of compassion burning. Eight in ten Americans report that their faith and beliefs help them to respect and assist other people. It is no wonder, then, that when, early on in our twenty-four-hour survey we asked people to define spirituality, they often spoke in terms of support to live a better life from something larger than themselves. Prayer and recourse to spiritual power will always fuel the most fruitful service and witness.

What shape will the witness of the church and religious community in America take?

An intriguing trend in how churches present themselves offers some clues. Suburban American churches and synagogues increasingly blend into their neighborhoods. More and more, the clean lines of brick and glass and steel emulate the most contemporary of office buildings. The "community center" ambiance, it is thought, eliminates obstacles to the seeking but church-shy neighbor. A cross or marquee may linger, but we see an accent on the horizontal, welcoming dimension, not a vertical transcendence.

It was not always so, of course. In older communities the church rose imposing through spire or arching walls of stone or brick. The church stood sentry over the village green of New England towns. Across the Great Plains, steeples loomed above squat buildings, competing only with water towers or grain elevators. Even older downtown churches, surrounded by skyscrapers, communicated a massive, commanding presence.

But in the closing decades of the twentieth century the landscape has changed, perhaps with more significance than most realize. Communities of faith and worship must continue to make their presence felt and known. Will the church continue to stay visible, not only through its architecture, but its deeds of goodness? Will it proclaim a transforming faith boldly and contagiously? Prophetically yet winsomely? A city set on a hill cannot be hid, said Jesus. Megachurches may indeed install their own coffee bars and spas and gyms; but through all the inwardly focused activities must come an outward posture, a studied gaze that looks beyond the walls and the stained glass to a wider world in need.

Most Americans live in an abundance that overflows their lives with more than enough to share with others, whether it be transplanted Sudanese or rural Appalachian farmers, whether it be a chaplain helping a college student explore the edges of doubt or a grandfather gently inviting his wayward grandson to join him at church. The witness must go on. And will, as we will demonstrate in our concluding chapter.

WHAT IS TO COME?: QUESTIONS FOR GOD

"The secularization of Europe has been going on for about 250 years. But I believe it has bottomed out. Modernity has collapsed and nobody believes in the autonomy of the human mind."

—JOHN STOTT

A N OPEN-ENDED QUESTION on the twenty-four-hour survey lifted a curtain on what Americans wonder about as they look ahead: "What would you like to ask God about your own life?" Some of the questions were understandably immediate: "Will my health improve? Will I live to enjoy a full life?" Another asked, "Will I have happiness?" Still another, from a thirty-eight-year-old man: "How long will I live?"

The perennial questions about evil and suffering came up, of course, like one from a nineteen-year-old receptionist: "Why does [God] let certain bad things happen—is there a good reason?"

Another asked the age-old, "Why do the innocent suffer?" Even more poignantly, said a seventy-eighty-year-old Southern Catholic, "I would like to ask him why he took my two wives away—and my dog who jumped off the deck during a storm." One baby boomer said she would ask, "Why is there so much violence and why have some people in my life been taken away by violence?" And not surprisingly, some wondered (or worried) about the afterlife: "I would like to know if I am on the right road to heaven." Or "What to do to get to heaven." One fifty-seven-year-old Methodist concluded, "I don't feel God should be asked these kinds of questions."

Especially striking was the number who revealed in their reflections the longing to know they were fulfilling God's purposes:

■ What am I supposed to do in this life—what is my purpose?
■ What [is God's] complete and perfect will . . . for my life[?]
■ Am I doing a good job spreading His word?
■ Why are things the way they are—can I change them for the better?

One response from a forty-eight-year-old factory supervisor especially struck us: "What [would] the future be like with [God's] guidance and wisdom?" This question has a larger scope, of course, than just one man's life. We wonder what the future will look like for our families, communities, world. A *USA Today/*Gallup poll conducted late in 1998 asked if in the year 2025 "life for average Americans will be better or worse than it is today." More than half, 53 percent, said "Better." And yet, when respondents replied to a question about it being easier or harder to "raise children to be good people" in 2025, a whopping 71 percent said "Harder."

Interesting to consider. But who can say with any certainty? No one knows the day or hour of the Second Advent and the close of history. And on even more immediate horizons we see through binoculars darkly. Could Americans living in the 1930s have even conceived of the next decade's Holocaust and world war? Who at the beginning of the 1980s could foresee the fall of the Berlin Wall at decade's end? Who would have imagined the grisly scenes of Columbine High School a year before they happened?

Still, we have maintained in this book the profit in looking ahead. While we have avoided the classical discipline of eschatology with all its controversies and theological intricacies, we also know that the trends we point to tell us important things about our world. We sometimes feel tempted, of course, not to bother to look ahead. We reason that the ways we are doing things will simply keep working. Each day's stresses of living and ministering seem more than enough. Indeed, Stephen Bertman in his book *Hyperculture* argues that an avalanche of change and information has taken us far beyond "future shock." We drift unanchored to the past, uncertain of the future, and live held simply by the power of now—at this instant. But there can be more.

As we have seen, examining Americans' faith commitment and spiritual practice can give us cause for thanksgiving and reason to roll up our sleeves for work. Prayer is up, yet many look at traditional Christianity and say, "You've had a go in Western culture, and now we want to try out other altars." Spirituality is "in" but the Cross for some seems antiquated, or perhaps just one path among many. We need to know the challenges facing us, the questions people ask, the wrong assumptions that lead them to dismiss what we try to share. We thereby gain clues to do what we do more intentionally, fruitfully.

Who Holds the Future?

But there is yet more to the story. In a real sense, this book has asked questions not just about American spiritual practice and belief and its future, but also questions of the One who holds the future. For to ask what spirituality and religion will look like in the twenty-first century is also to ponder the ways of God. Given the conviction that God is at work in human history, then, we have kept in mind not only sociological patterns, paths, and likely scenarios, but have worked with the assumption that a larger hand guides the processes and patterns we discern.

And historically God's work does seem to have "seasons." We see biblical revivals of moral loyalty and prayer and worship in the reigns of Hezekiah and Josiah. We see Israel's commitment wane, then wax. The New Testament account of the early church's Pentecost suggests how God may choose to work more visibly in some areas than in others. The long sweep of the church's history is filled with both dismal failure and heroic sanctity, corrupt institutions and Great Awakenings. But through it all, the work of redemption continues to flourish. Wherever and whenever prayer for God's reviving work increases, we believe, so will the response. Where a people turn to Him for strength to do good, we believe, abilities will come. More will be done than could be done with human energy alone.

> The long sweep of the church's history is filled with both dismal failure and heroic sanctity, corrupt institutions and Great Awakenings. But through it all, the work of redemption continues to flourish. Wherever and whenever prayer for God's reviving work increases, we believe, so will the response.

Such convictions help. Yes, there are signs of decline among many churches. Granted, secularism's hollow legacy still hovers over much of our life. And massive social problems such as abortion and poverty and environmental degradation drain our life and threaten our future. But a long view will help us gird our loins for undaunted action. If the institutional church is seeing tough days, perhaps small groups and cell-based churches will thrive and take on new life. If old denominational structures die, then Christ, who promises, "Lo, I am with you always," will be sure to enable the creation of new ones. Perhaps in the coming century the church may experience increased hostility from the wider culture. But we think of deeper questions: Is God leading His people into new opportunities? Will prayer guide us into a time or renewed vigor and engagement with culture's ills? Will the church lose its insularity and turn out members to minister in penitentiaries and crack houses and streets crowded with the homeless?

Few things seem clearer than that God will not stop working out His purposes. It can be argued that the ultimate significance of renewals and revivals becomes clear only with time, usually with hindsight. But foresight has a place too. Sanctified hope and an urgent commitment to "pray in" the threshold of a millennium will only make us that much more open to what God wants to do. Is our culture's rediscovery of spirituality just a fad? Possibly. But in all our discernment and effort we continue to press the question, "What is God up to?" Can we ready ourselves for another Great Awakening? The best news of all is that we are not alone as we peer ahead. As United Methodist Tex Sample writes:

> *The Spirit is loose in the world, and the Word of God through which and by which the cosmos was created is now moving in the world to transform the world. This is profoundly good news. The Spirit of Christ precedes us into the world. This Spirit is already at work in any society, any culture, any lifestyle, and absolutely nothing can stop this redemptive, liberative, and transformative power. The task of the church, then, is to seek out the Spirit of Christ, to discern the current of saving work, to affirm—wherever it appears— authentic, qualitative life and to call into question the bondage, illusion, and death of a twisted world. This means that we are not called to go anywhere where Christ has not already gone ahead to open the way, so that we are able to go confident in the moving power of the Spirit. This is a bracing framework in which to pursue ministry among the lifestyles of any culture, including our own.* [1]

The Most Religious Century?

We live in perilous times at this threshold of a new century, but also times of expectancy and faith. Our world will continue to make extraordinary advances in the years ahead—vast leaps in medicine, transportation, communications. Progress is speeding up, exponentially, it seems. But people the world over seem to realize that humankind cannot solve all its problems, not when left to its own devices. Karl Marx wrote in the nineteenth century that religion was the opiate of the people, that it would fade as education increased.

The twentieth century, of course, proved him dead wrong. The vast majority of people worldwide adhere to some religion, and international Gallup surveys reveal that a large majority of the world continues to believe in a supreme being or universal spirit. Writes theologian and commentator Michael Novak, "At the millennium, secular humanism shows its limits. . . . You may be sure that the twenty-first century will be the most religious in five hundred years. . . . We have come through a long and bloody century, and something new is stirring everywhere. It is none too soon." [2]

Indeed, says historian Paul Johnson, perhaps by the last decade of the twentieth century people have learned some larger lessons. When he wrote, he said, it was not yet clear if the evils behind the century's "catastrophic failures and tragedies—the rise of moral relativism, the decline of personal responsibility, the repudiation of Judeo-Christian values, . . . the arrogant belief that men and women could solve all the mysteries of the universe by their own unaided intellect"—were being eradicated. On that eventuality, he concluded, "would depend the chance of the twenty-first century becoming, by contrast, an age of hope for mankind." [3]

With such recognition of our limits may come an even greater surge of interest in spirituality, an openness to a fresh breeze of the Holy Spirit, blowing us where He will, leading us into a world of desperate need and great promise.

FAST FACTS ABOUT AMERICA'S SPIRITUALITY

(Unless otherwise noted, numbers represent percentages of adults)

GOD AND SPIRITUALITY

Believe in God or a universal spirit	96%
Believe Jesus Christ is God or the Son of God	84%
Believe in heaven	90%
Rate their chance of going to heaven as good	77%
Believe in hell	73%
Say their chance of going to hell is excellent	23%
Experience in their lives a need for spiritual growth	82%
Say they have a personal relationship with God	80%

Believe in astrology	23%
Say there are angels	72%
Believe the Bible is the inspired Word of God but should not be taken literally	48%
Say they have attended church at least once in the last seven days	43%
Pray to a supreme being such as God	75%
Pray at least daily	75%

The United States is unique in that it has one of the highest levels of formal education in the world, and at the same time, one of the highest levels of religious faith.

Seven in ten Americans say their faith has changed significantly, with equal proportions saying it came about as a result of a lot of thought and discussion, and as a result of a strong emotional experience.

How do Americans most often nourish and strengthen their religious faith? Through prayer, helping others, attending religious services, and reading the Bible.

RELIGION AND SOCIETY

Say religion can solve all or most of today's problems	61%
Believe religion is increasing its influence on America	31%
Think clergy could have a great deal of influence in raising ethical standards	68%

Say their own religious leaders are the people   7%
    most likely to influence their political views

Say they are satisfied with the care being   15%
    given to the poor and needy in America

Local churches top a list of twenty-four organizations that the public believes are trying to improve city life.

Eighteen percent of adults are conservatives in terms of their religious ideology; 47 percent moderates; and 19 percent liberals.

Of eight professions tested to determine the public's perceptions of their status, physicians and the clergy emerge as the most prestigious. The public, however, approves of much higher pay for physicians than for the clergy.

THE CHURCH AND THE YOUNG

Teens who say they believe in God   95%

Teens who say God loves them   93%

Teens who believe in heaven   91%

College freshmen who expect to major   < 1%
    in theology or religion, earn a divinity
    degree, or pursue a religious vocation

Teens who pray when alone   74%

Teens who have a great deal of interest   64%
    in discussing the existence of God

Most Americans say the home is the most important

place for the religious training of youth, far more than say church or school.

Homes where religion plays a central role produce persons whose future homes in all likelihood also will be religiously oriented.

RELIGIOUS AFFILIATION

Claim membership in a church, synagogue, or other religious body	69%
State a religious preference	92%
State Protestant as their preference	58%
State Catholic as their preference	25%
Describe themselves as born again or evangelical	41%
Describe themselves as belonging to the religious right	18%
State Islam, Hinduism, or Buddhism as their preference	< 1% for each

Eight in ten Americans consider themselves to be Christians. According to the most stringent question we have devised to date, six in ten completely agree that the only assurance of eternal life is a personal faith in Jesus Christ.

FAITH AND THE FUTURE

Believe that people will be more religious	48%
Believe that within twenty-five years we will experience an environmental crisis	49%

Believe that it will be harder to raise   71%
   children to be good

For the first time in a half-century of surveys on Americans' top national concerns, a 1999 poll revealed that "ethics, morality, and family decline" led the list at 18 percent.

Just over half (51 percent) say they expect religion to become more important to them in the future.

2

THE TWENTY-FOUR-HOUR SPIRITUAL PRACTICE SURVEY

PHILOSOPHY OF LIFE?

Do you have a philosophy of life, or rules that guide your daily life?

Yes	81%
No	18%
DK/NA	1%

DK = Don't know
NA = No answer

What is your philosophy of life? (selected responses)

Golden Rule: Do unto others as you would have them do unto you

Try to be the best person I can be

Center my life in Jesus Christ; try to follow/be like Him

Be guided by the Bible, the Ten Commandments, my
religion

Seek to discover and do God's will

Live life to the fullest; seek happiness

Be true to myself

My faith in Christ

FEEL NEED TO EXPERIENCE SPIRITUAL GROWTH?

Do you feel the need in your life to experience spiritual
growth?

Yes	78%
No	22%

DEFINING SPIRITUALITY

What does the word *spirituality* mean to you? (selected
responses and ranked in order of frequency of mention)

Belief in God/seeking to grow closer to God

Belief in a higher power, something beyond oneself/
sense of awe and mystery in the universe

Inner peace/state of mind

Seeking to be a good person/lead a good life

Seeking the inner self/the being within your body/the
essence of your personal being/evolving into a whole
spirit/experiencing spiritual side of the natural order

Reach human potential/to affirm sense of personal
worth

What has been learned from upbringing, school, church, the Bible

A mystical bond with other people

Sense of right and wrong/to know who you are and what you are doing is right

A calmness in my life

Going to church and being a good person

HOW DO YOU THINK OF "SPIRITUALITY"?

Do you think of "spirituality" more in a personal and individual sense, or more in terms of organized religion and church doctrine?

In a personal and individual sense	72%
In terms of organized religion and church doctrine	21%
DK/NA	7%

PATTERN IN SPIRITUAL LIFE IN LAST 24 HOURS?

Has there been a pattern in your spiritual life during the last twenty-four hours, with spiritual highs and lows?

Yes	35%
No	60%
DK/NA	5%

WHAT WAS EXPERIENCED?

At any time in the last twenty-four hours did you experience the following?

Loneliness	16%

Guilt	10%
A feeling that people don't understand you	10%
A feeling that life is empty or meaningless	6%
Fear of death and dying	4%
A feeling that you are not loved	3%
DK/NA	68%

EXPERIENCE INDESCRIBABLE JOY?

In the last twenty-four hours did you happen, at any point, to experience indescribable joy—joy that cannot be put into words?

| Yes | 31% |
| No | 69% |

DARK MOMENTS

Were there any dark moments of discouragement or despair?

| Yes | 22% |
| No | 78% |

TURN TO GOD AT SUCH TIMES?

Did you happen to turn to God or a higher power, the inner self, or Jesus Christ at these times?

| Yes | 53%* |
| No | 46% |

DK/NA   1%

   *Results based on total sample

BELIEF ABOUT GOD?

Please tell me which statement comes closest to expressing what you believe about God.

I know God really exists and I have no doubts about it	79%
I don't believe in a personal God, but I do believe in a higher power of some kind	12%
I don't know whether there is a God and I don't believe there is any way to find out	3%
I find myself believing in God some of the time but not at others	3%
I don't believe in God	2%
DK/NA	1%

TRUST IN GOD?

How much trust would you say you have in God—absolute trust, quite a lot, a fair amount, little trust, or no trust at all?

Absolute trust	61%
Quite a lot	20%
A fair amount	12%
Little trust	2%

No trust at all   4%

DK/NA   1%

PART OF CHRISTIAN TRADITION?

Do you consider yourself a part of the Christian religious tradition, some other non-Christian religious tradition, or no religious tradition in particular?

Christian religious tradition   83%

Some other non-Christian religious tradition   6%

No tradition   10%

DK/NA   1%

QUESTIONS LIKE TO ASK GOD?

What is the most important question you, as a Christian, would like to ask God about your own life? (asked of those who identified themselves as Christians; selected responses and ranked in order of frequency of mention)

Am I pleasing God? Going in the right direction? Worthy of His love?

Why are there problems in the world? Why do the innocent suffer?

Will I see heaven? What do I need to do to get to heaven?

What is God's ultimate purpose? What is His plan for my life? Why has He not revealed Himself to me sooner?

How can I encourage my children to walk with God?

How can I grow in faith?

What will the future be like—will I find happiness? Will my health improve? How long will I live?

WHO IS JESUS CHRIST?

Which one of these statements comes closest to your beliefs?

God or Jesus Christ gives us strength to deal with problems, to call on our God-given resources	59%
God or Jesus Christ or a higher power intervenes directly in my life	25%
It is strictly a matter of mind over matter—God is not involved	12%
DK/NA	4%

KNOW ABOUT—OR KNOW—JESUS CHRIST?

Which statement comes closer to what you believe?

I KNOW Jesus Christ	56%
I KNOW ABOUT Jesus Christ	43%
DK/NA	1%

RELY ON SELF—OR GOD?

Do you rely more on yourself to solve the problems of life, or more on an outside power, such as God?

Rely more on myself	53%
Rely more on an outside power such as God	41%

DK/NA   6%

SENSE OF GOD'S PRESENCE?

At any point during the last twenty-four hours, did you have a strong sense of God's presence?

Yes   49%

No   47%

DK/NA   4%

HIGHER POWER/GOD HELP YOU GET THROUGH?

Do you believe God/a higher power/or your inner self helps you get through each day?

Yes   91%

No   9%

SENSE OF BEING PART OF GOD'S PLAN?

In the last twenty-four hours, did you have any sense of being part of God's plan or purposes?

Yes   59%

No   39%

DK/NA   2%

SENSE OF GOD BEING LOVING?

At any point in your day did you have a sense of God being loving?

Yes   70%

No   27%

DK/NA   3%

SENSE OF GOD BEING ANGRY?
At any point in your day did you have a sense of God being angry?

Yes   9%

No   89%

DK/NA   2%

MODERN LIFE LEAVES YOU TOO BUSY FOR GOD?
Do you sometimes feel modern life leaves you too busy to enjoy God or pray as you would like?

Yes   51%

No   49%

PRAYER IN LAST 24 HOURS?
During the last twenty-four hours, did you happen to pray?

Yes   67%

No   33%

WHAT DID YOU PRAY FOR?
How, if at all, would you say your prayers related to your life during the last twenty-four hours? (selected responses and ranked in order of frequency of mention)

Seeking guidance from God

Praying is an ongoing part of my daily life

Thanksgiving to God

Parenting

Seeking God's protection

Prayer gives me comfort, sense of peace

To find out what God expects of me

Prayers for friends

Prayed for world peace

Prayed for people I knew

Thanked God for all the gifts He has given me

Prayed for my family

We prayed for rain and got it

DID YOU GO OUT OF WAY TO HELP SOMEONE?

During the last twenty-four hours, was there an occasion when you went out of your way to help someone else because of spiritual or faith reasons?

Yes	45%
No	54%
DK/NA	1%

GIFTS/ABILITITES FROM GOD

Do you believe you have gifts or abilities from God?

Yes	79%
No	16%
DK/NA	5%

CHANCE TO USE GIFTS?

Did you have a chance to use these gifts or abilities during the last twenty-four hours?

Yes	74%
No	25%
DK	1%

SEEKING TO GROW IN RELIGIOUS FAITH?

Would you say that you are seeking to grow in your religious faith, or not?

Yes	76%
No	24%

TO WHAT EXTENT GROWING IN FAITH?

To what extent—a great deal, somewhat or hardly at all, or not at all?

Great deal	57%
Somewhat	40%
Not at all	1%
DK/NA	3%

SUPPORT OF OTHERS IMPORTANT TO FAITH?

Are the presence and support of others important to your religious faith or personal life?

Yes	69%
No	30%
DK/NA	1%

TALK ABOUT RELIGIOUS FAITH IN WORKPLACE?
Did you have occasion to talk about your religious faith in the workplace?

Yes	48%
No	52%

IN LAST 24 HOURS: WHICH OF THESE DID YOU DO?
In the last twenty-four hours—that is, between this time today and this time yesterday—did you happen to do any of the following?

In last twenty-four hours . . .

Prayed at a meal	55%
Talked to someone about God or some aspect of my faith or spirituality	51%
Shared my faith	44%
Read the Bible	36%
Read books or articles with spiritual themes	32%
Counseled someone from a spiritual perspective	25%
Watched/listened to religious radio/TV	24%
Spoke out on a national issue out of my religious conviction	22%
Attended a prayer service or Bible study or worship group	15%
Listened to cassette tapes with spiritual themes	15%

Called a psychic hot line or read my horoscope	5%
Used the Internet to research or explore a matter of religious faith	3%
Visited computer Web sites related to churches or that contain spiritual themes	2%

FIRST THING THOUGHT ABOUT—MORNING?

(see chapter 3 for selected responses)
Do you happen to recall the first thing you thought about when you woke up this morning?

Yes	78%

LAST THING THOUGHT ABOUT—EVENING?

(see chapter 3 for selected responses)
Do you happen to recall the last thing you thought about when you went to bed last night?

Yes	54%

CHURCH MEMBERSHIP

Do you happen to be a member of a church, synagogue, mosque, or other organized religious group?

Yes	64%

FREQUENCY OF CHURCH ATTENDANCE

How often do you attend religious services?

At least once a week	44%
Almost every week	10%
About once a month	8%

Seldom   29%

Never   9%

NOTE: *The results of this survey are based on a telephone interview with a randomly selected national sample of one hundred adults, eighteen years and older, conducted in July 1999. For results based on this sample (one hundred interviews), one can say with 95 percent confidence that the maximum error attributable to sampling and other random effects is plus or minus 11 percentage points. In addition to sampling error, question wording and practical difficulties in conducting surveys can introduce error or bias into the findings of public opinion polls.*

ENDNOTES

Introduction

1. Faith Popcorn, *Clicking* (New York: HarperCollins, 1996), 132.

2. Tom Sine, *Mustard Seed versus McWorld* (Grand Rapids, Mich.: Baker, 1999), 11.

3. Lisa Miller, "God Goes Online," *Wall Street Journal,* March 26, 1999, W1.

4. I was introduced to this phrase by Leonard Sweet in *SoulTsunami* (Grand Rapids, Mich.: Zondervan, 1999), 24.

Chapter 1: America's Epic Soul Quest

1. Nancy Gibbs, "In Sorrow and Disbelief," *Time,* May 3, 1999.

2. Ibid.

3. Stephen Carter, *The Culture of Disbelief* (New York: Basic Books/HarperCollins, 1993).

4. Mark I. Pinsky, "'The Simpsons': Sinners or Saints," *Tennessean,* August 24, 1999), 2D.

5. For information on the Princeton Religion Research Center or its newsletter and other publications: e-mail: marie_swirsky@gallup.com; Web site: http://www.prrc.com; phone: 609/279-2255; fax: 609/924-0228; address: P.O. Box 389, Hulfish Street, Princeton, NJ 08542.

6. Jack Miles, "Religion Makes a Comeback," *New York Times Magazine,* December 12, 1997.

7. David N. Elkins, "It's What's Missing in Mental Health," *Psychology Today,* September/October 1999, 45.

8. Ibid.

9. Robert Wuthnow, *After Heaven* (Berkeley, Calif.: University of California Press, 1998), 1.

10. George Gallup, Jr., and Timothy Jones, *The Saints Among Us* (Wilton, Conn.: Morehouse, 1992).

11. Quoted in Gary M. Burge, "The Greatest Story Never Read," *Christianity Today,* August 9, 1999, 45.

12. Ray Waddle, "Leaving Religion Out When Considering This Century," *Tennessean,* July 18, 1999, 2D.

13. David S. Broder, "The National Mood Has Darkened," *Washington Post,* June 30, 1999, A31.

14. See Cornelius Plantinga, Jr., "Dancing the Edge of Mystery," *Books and Culture,* September/October 1999, 16.

15. Statistic from the National Law Center on Homelessness and Poverty, 1999.

16. Frank Gibney, "The Kids Got in the Way," *Time,* August 23, 1999, 29.

17. George Gallup, Jr., with Wendy Plump, *Growing Up Scared in America—And What the Experts Say Parents Can Do About It* (Princeton, N.J.: Princeton Religion Research Center, 1995). See also George Gallup, Jr., with Wendy Plump,

Growing Up Scared in America—And What the Experts Say Parents Can Do About It (Harrisburg, Pa.: Morehouse, 1996).

18. Mark Buchanan, "Trapped in the Cult of the Next Thing," *Christianity Today,* September 6, 1999, 63, 65.

19. Wuthnow, *After Heaven*, 10.

20. Ibid., 11.

21. Leonard Sweet, *SoulTsunami* (Grand Rapids, Mich.: Zondervan, 1999), 420.

22. Ibid.

23. Garry Wills, *Saint Augustine* (New York: Penguin, 1999), 6.

24. Dave Henderson, *Culture Shift* (Grand Rapids, Mich.: Baker, 1999).

Chapter 2: The New Spirituality

1. Quoted in Leonard Sweet, *SoulTsunami* (Grand Rapids, Mich.: Zondervan, 1999), 408.

2. Sophy Burnham, *A Book of Angels* (New York: Ballantine, 1990), xii.

3. Eugene Peterson, *Subversive Spirituality* (Grand Rapids, Mich.: William B. Eerdmans, 1994, 1997), 33.

4. Ibid., 34.

5. Robert N. Bellah, et al., *Habits of the Heart* (New York: Harper & Row, 1985), 221.

6. Patricia Hampl, "Introduction," in Philip Zaleski, ed., *The Best Spiritual Writing 1998* (San Francisco: HarperSanFrancisco, 1998), xxii.

7. Phyllis Tickle, *God-Talk in America* (New York: Crossroad, 1997), 1-2.

8. Neale Donald Walsch, *Conversations with God* (New York: Putnam, 1996).

9. L. Gregory Jones, "Spirituality Lite: Thomas Moore's Misguided Care of the Soul," *Christian Century,* November 6, 1996, 1,072, 1,074.

10. Eugene Peterson, *Answering God* (San Francisco: Harper & Row, 1980), 87.

11. Dallas Willard, *The Divine Conspiracy* (San Francisco: HarperSanFrancisco, 1998), 38, 41.

12. Gustav Niebuhr, "Religion Journal," *New York Times,* July 24, 1999.

13. *Utne Reader,* July-August 1998.

14. Anne Lamott, *Traveling Mercies* (New York: Pantheon, 1999), 41.

15. Jeremiah Creedon, "God with a Million Faces," *Utne Reader,* July-August, 1998, 47.

16. Ibid.

17. Gary M. Burge, "The Greatest Story Never Read," *Christianity Today,* August 9, 1999, 45.

18. Ibid.

19. Ibid., 47.

20. Robert Wuthnow, "How Small Groups Are Transforming Our Lives," *Christianity Today,* February 7, 1994, 22.

21. Ibid.

22. Ibid.

Chapter 3: A Day in the Life: How Americans Talk with God

1. Andy Dappen, "When Less Becomes More," *Hemispheres,* November 1997, 155, quoted in Tom Sine, *Mustard Seed versus McWorld* (Grand Rapids, Mich.: Baker, 1999), 90.

2. Quoted in Robert Wuthnow, *After Heaven* (Berkeley, Calif.: University of California Press, 1998), 134.

3. Robert Coles, *The Secular Mind* (Princeton: Princeton University Press, 1999), 34.

4. Barnes & Noble Online (www.barnesandnoble.com), July 26, 1999.

5. Martin E. Marty, "Sightings," Public Religion Project (prp-info@publicreligionproj.org), May 14, 1999.

6. Faith Popcorn, *Clicking* (New York: HarperCollins, 1996), 136.

7. Marty, "Sightings."

8. David W. Chen, "Fitting the Lord into Work's Tight Schedules," *New York Times,* November 29, 1997.

9. Robert Coles, *The Secular Mind,* 36, 38.

10. Kenneth Woodward, "Talking to God," *Newsweek,* January 6, 1992, 39.

11. Rick Hamlin, *Meeting God on the A Train* (San Francisco: HarperSanFrancisco, 1997), 4.

12. Nina Siegal, "Squeezing in Soul Time; New Yorkers Take Five from the Workday to Feed the Spirit," *New York Times,* April 4, 1999.

13. Tim Padgett, ". . . And to the Latin Mass," *Time,* June 7, 1999.

14. David Van Biema, "Back to the Yarmulke," *Time,* June 7, 1999.

15. See, for example, biochemist Michael Behe's book *Darwin's Black Box.*

16. See Richard Foster, *Streams of Living Water* (San Francisco: HarperSanFrancisco, 1998).

17. Richard Kew, from "The Great Spirituality Boom," a speech delivered January 1997.

18. Wuthnow, *After Heaven,* 134.

Chapter 4: A Day in the Life:
How Americans Need and Help Others

1. George Barna, *The Second Coming of the Church* (Nashville: Word, 1998), 3.

2. George Gallup, Jr., and Timothy Jones, *The Saints Among Us* (Wilton, Conn.: Morehouse, 1992).

3. Robert Wuthnow, *After Heaven* (Berkeley, Calif.: University of California Press, 1998), 192.

4. Thomas Merton, *The Seven Storey Mountain* (New York: Harcourt Brace Jovanovich, 1948), 415.

5. Barna, 190.

6. Donald E. Miller, *Reinventing American Protestantism* (Berkeley, Calif.: University of Southern California Press, 1997), 111-112.

7. Michael G. Maudlin, "God's Contractor," *Christianity Today,* June 14, 1999, 44.

8. See http://www.missionamerica.org.

9. ReligionToday.com, July 27, 1999. See http://www.religionto-day.com.

Chapter 5: Three Groups to Watch

1. Tim Stafford, "The Criminologist Who Discovered Churches," *Christianity Today,* June 14, 1999, 34.

2. Brook Latimer, "Latino America," *Newsweek,* July 12, 1999, 4-8.

3. See http://ourworld.compuserve.com/homepages/amadrid.

4. Quoted in Leonard Sweet, *SoulTsunami* (Grand Rapids, Mich.: Zondervan, 1999), 384.

5. Mars Hill Productions, *Generation* (study guide to the video series of the same name) (Missouri City, Texas: Mars Hill Productions, 1997), 62.

6. Quoted in Wendy Murray Zoba, "The Class of '00," *Christianity Today,* February 3, 1997, 18.

7. Ibid.

8. Ibid.

9. Jimmy and Rosalynn Carter, *Everything to Gain* (New York: Random House, 1997).

10. John Leland, "Savior of the Streets," *Newsweek,* June 1, 1998.

Chapter 6: What Should We Do?: Working Spirituality Down Deep

1. Eugene Peterson, *Subversive Spirituality* (Grand Rapids, Mich.: Wm. B. Eerdmans, 1994, 1997), 36.

2. Ibid., 36-37.

3. Mike Regele with Mark Schulz, *Death of the Church* (Grand Rapids, Mich.: Zondervan, 1995), 80.

4. Joel Belz editorial, *World,* n.d.

5. James K. Hampton, "The Challenge of Postmodernism," *Youthworker,* January/February 1999, 20.

6. Cornelius Plantinga, Jr., "Dancing the Edge of Mystery," *Books and Culture,* September/October 1999, 16.

7. Lillian Daniel, "I Love to Tell the Story to Those Who Know It Least," *Christianity Today,* August 9, 1999, 50.

8. Eugene Peterson, *Answering God* (San Francisco: Harper & Row, 1989), 18.

9. M. Robert Mulholland, Jr., *Invitation to a Journey* (Downers Grove, Ill.: InterVarsity, 1993).

10. Andy Drietcer, in "Traveling Without a Map," Chris de Vinck, ed., *Nouwen Then* (Grand Rapids, Mich.: Zondervan, 1999), 90-91.

11. George Barna, *The Second Coming of the Church* (Nashville: Word, 1998), 6.

12. Helene Stapinski, "Y Not Love?" *American Demographics,* February 1999.

13. Barna, *The Second Coming of the Church,* 190.

14. Ernest L. Boyer, "The Third Wave of School Reform," *Christianity Today,* September 22, 1989, 16.

15. Brad Sargent, "The Tornado of Transitions." For information contact the author at Golden Gate Baptist Theological Seminary, Box 217, 201 Seminary Drive, Mill Valley, CA 94941, or BradSargent@ggbts.edu.

16. Tom Beaudoin, *Virtual Faith* (San Francisco: Jossey-Bass, 1998), 21.

17. James Emery White, "Two Pastors in a Demographic Debate: Should the Church Target Generations?" *Leadership,* Spring 1999, 104.

18. Garth Bolinder, "No, So the Church May Be One," Ibid.

19. Michael Slaughter, *Out on the Edge* (Nashville: Abingdon, 1998), 39.

20. Ibid., 23.

21. Ibid.

22. Terry Teachout, "How We Get That Story," *Wall Street Journal,* August 6, 1999.

23. Patricia Hampl, "Introduction," Philip Zaleski, ed., *The Best Spiritual Writing 1998* (San Francisco: HarperSan-Francisco, 1998), xiii.

24. Lisa Miller, "God Goes Online," *Wall Street Journal,* March 26, 1999.

25. Michael Dertouzos, *What Will Be* (New York: HarperEdge, 1997), 201.

Chapter 7: Where Should We Go?: Reaching Beyond Our Walls

1. John Stackhouse, "Why Our Friends Won't Stop, Look, and Listen," *Christianity Today,* February 3, 1997, 51.

2. Tom Sine, *Mustard Seed versus McWorld* (Grand Rapids, Mich.: Baker, 1999), 18.

3. Brad Sargent, "The Tornado of Transitions," For information contact the author at Golden Gate Baptist Theological Seminary, Box 217, 201 Seminary Drive, Mill Valley, CA 94941, or BradSargent@ggbts.edu.

4. Source unavailable.

5. Stackhouse, *Christianity Today,* 49.

6. Material taken from the Alpha Web site: http://www.alpha.org.uk/index.htm.

Chapter 8: What Is to Come?: Questions for God

1. Tex Sample, source unavailable.

2. Michael Novak, "The Most Religious Century," *New York Times,* May 24, 1998.

3. Paul Johnson, *Modern Times: The World from the Twenties to the Nineties* (New York: HarperPerennial, 1983, 1991), 784.